DREAM SMALLER

DREAM SMALLER

A REACTION AGAINST THE IDEA THAT WOMEN CAN'T 'HAVE IT ALL'

DREW CAITLIN DUDLEY

NEW DEGREE PRESS

DREAM SMALLER

A Reaction Against the Idea that Women Can't 'Have It All'

ISBN   978-1-64137-319-7   *Paperback*

          978-1-64137-618-1   *Ebook*

For my family who has supported and cultivated my tendency to dream big since I was a little girl. Thank you for being my cheerleaders, shoulders to lean on, champions, and biggest fans. Without you all, none of this would be possible.

Contents

"One of the lessons that I grew up with was to always stay true to yourself and never let what somebody else says distract you from your goals. And so when I hear about negative and false attacks, I really don't invest any energy in them, because I know who I am."

—MICHELLE OBAMA

Introduction

Dear Reader,

First and foremost... I appreciate you. Thank you for picking up this book.

Frankly, I wish we were having this conversation in person, because I desperately want to see your reaction to the story I am about to tell you.

It's one hundred percent true (although names and selected details have been changed to protect the guilty), and it's the reason this book is in your hands.

How it all began...

I was a leader of an organization called the Husky Sales Club. Every week we were so lucky to be blessed with real-world high-level sales professionals who took the time to help us grow both personally and professionally. For a year, it was my role to curate those speakers and combine efforts with them to deliver relevant and inspiring talks. There is magic in being able to soak up every ounce of knowledge they have and each piece of advice they give about their experiences in the business world. I idolized these speakers and am so grateful that I got to personally network with them.

It was a truly special experience, and I found many a professional mentor through my role.

Before each meeting, I got fifteen minutes with the speakers all to myself as they prepared to present. We ran through logistics, had interesting conversations, and often they inquired about me and my professional goals:

- "What industries am I interested in?"
- "Do I already have a job lined up?"
- "As the speaker, can I eat the Chipotle that's catered or is that just for the attendees?"

One Tuesday night, I brought in the Vice President of Sales at this high-growth tech company located right in the heart of downtown Seattle. He came in prepared to talk about the three factors to success for anyone just starting out in their career. Before the meeting, he asked me about my plans post-grad. I proudly said that I already had my dream job at probably the only company that could keep me in Seattle.

He congratulated me, and then asked a ringer of a follow-up question, "What's your ten-year plan?"

I laughed uncomfortably.

That ten-year timeline was too far into the future for me. I barely knew what I would be doing next *week*... let alone 520 weeks from now. I paused before responding and gave myself a little internal pep talk—I do this a lot—that went a little something like this... *Wow! Okay. Ten-year plan? This is your ten years; you can make it anything you want it to be! What do you love now that you still want to be doing ten years from now?*

"I want to be a regularly published fiction author," I began. "Right now, I'm a creative writing major. It feeds my soul, and it's something I can get lost in. I want to be on track to be a senior-level sales executive for a high-growth organization because I have a passion for business and helping people."

I paused then decided to give him the whole story, "And I also want to be starting a cute little family who loves to travel with me at some point in there, too. So yes, I'd say being an author, moving up the ladder in my sales career, and starting a family are all in my ten-year plan."

He looked down, offered me a half-laugh, and shook his head. "Those are some lofty goals you've got there. You might want to think about scaling back a bit." He paused, then continued, "Maybe you should dream a little smaller. I don't know anyone who's hit their ten-year plan..."

Dream Smaller.

The words rang loudly in my ears.

He kept talking but I couldn't process what he was saying. I was stuck on two words:

Dream. Smaller.

It was my job to stand there and chat with him until it was time for me to introduce him to the group. I had a fake smile on my face and was nodding intently at what he had to say because I had to. This was the Vice President of Sales at a company I knew and respected. If he said my ten-year plan was trying to accomplish too much then maybe he was right?

I didn't know! I had to think about it...

For the rest of the meeting, I felt like I needed to ask the perfect question and contribute in the most productive way to the conversation just to get a smidgen of his approval. Who was I to think I knew better than he did?

That conversation—those two words—stayed with me. Was he right? Did I need to dream smaller? On the walk home that Tuesday night, I kept playing our conversation on repeat in my head. *Ten-year plan. Writer. Salesperson. Mom. Dream smaller.* I swear I went through a strange three-step version of grief. Okay, that sounds a little dramatic but seriously... I was mourning the death of the life I hadn't even had a chance to live yet. I moved from denial into bargaining with myself about what was "more realistic."

Okay. Well, if I want to be a regularly published author, that will probably take up most of my time so I will probably have to quit my sales role because the hours are too rigid. If I want to be really successful in sales and move up quickly, I will probably be so busy I won't have time for a family until at least fifteen years from now. He might be right. But what I really want is to be able to look at my husband and our beautiful kiddos and fist bump him and say, "We made that!" So that should take top priority, and I will probably quit my demanding sales job but at least that will give me some time to write a little bit!

But f*ck that!

I was not just angry; I was fuming. Seriously, you probably could have seen the steam pouring out of my ears. This guy didn't know me. He sure as hell didn't know my work ethic... and *I was not going to let him weigh my passions and deliver the verdict on what I could accomplish in my life!*

What did other women think?

While I simmered, I turned to the female mentors in my life. I felt pathetic going to them after this conversation. Part of me thought they would reaffirm what that VP of Sales told me. Boy, was I wrong.

Those two words, *Dream Smaller*, shocked every single woman I retold this story to. They had second-hand rage for me. It was awesome and inspiring and altogether overwhelming to hear how other women reacted to his words. They were saddened but not surprised that I had this experience. Many experienced a similar instance in which they were told to make themselves smaller than they aspired to be—and not just by men!

The worst part of all of this is that he probably doesn't even remember the conversation. But I do. It lit a fire in me to prove him wrong and, in the same vein, find the women who have created a life for themselves that they find fulfilling. The women in these pages do not 'have it all' as measured against a societal yardstick. Yet, they have designed lives for themselves that allow them to explore and to be involved in the most important areas.

Pearls of Wisdom for All Seasons of Life

Come to this book as you are. If you are a young woman (like me!) just starting out your career and trying to discover how others have navigated the road before you then right on! If you are a mom dealing with the unique challenge of balancing your career with your family then you got this! For each season of your life, there is a story for you within the pages of this book. You might be someone who is as equally committed to your passion as you are to your job. Where are my triathletes and home brewers at? You might be a dreamer with a side hustle or a passionate volunteer. There are pearls of wisdom in this book for all of you. The strategies and tools the women within these pages used to create the life they are living may not be the exact same tools that you need in your own life, but they do have a spark of magic. Think of them as a jumping-off point for your own dreams and aspirations.

I hope they cause you to think deeply about your passions and goals and how they play out in your life.

- **Hope** - My *hope* is that you realize your own potential.
- **Think** - I want you to *think* about what is truly important and fulfilling in your life.
- **Passions** -I want you to uncover what you are passionate about... and then go out and fiercely pursue it!
- **Goals** - I want you to continue to strive toward your goals.
- **Life** - You only have one life; make sure you live it to the fullest!

As we explore together, I hope you find inspiration. I hope you discover your inner strength. I hope you are able to visualize your desired life. Draw on the inspiration in this book to be proactive in your own life. Find the power that comes from being vulnerable. Your desired life is the life you want to live. Then, once you visualize that pot of gold at the end of the rainbow, take active steps to chase it.

While we acknowledge the learning moments born out of failures and together celebrate the successes, I hope you are inspired to be proactive in your own life and see the beauty in becoming resilient. As we discuss what it means to be a mother and a friend, I *hope* you see there is strength in being vulnerable and courage in asking for help. Through the story I just shared with you and the stories of other women who have been told to be a smaller, more palatable version of themselves, I hope you visualize the life you want to live and take active steps to cultivate it for yourself.

Each story in this book reaffirms for me that there is nothing more powerful than women helping women. I am gifting all of this wisdom to you, Reader, because not sharing it with you would be selfish. I am so passionate about dreaming big that I want these words to echo louder than the voice in your life telling you to Dream Smaller.

Dream on... and Dream BIGGER. I believe in you.

With sincere love and appreciation,

Drew

Part One

Having It All
in Good Time

Chapter 1

Having It All

If your reaction to the phrase 'Have It All' is immediate distrust, scoffing, disgust, or the urge to set this book down... STOP! Don't do it yet. Hear me out. If, after my explanation, you decide that you hold fast to your well-founded beliefs, then you can donate this book to the local library.

So, what does it mean to 'Have It All' within the context of this book? It means that you have designed your life in a way that makes space for you to accomplish the specific goals and dreams that are most important to you. It doesn't take a degree in engineering to divine the equation to create this 'Having It All' outcome for yourself. Here, I will give it to you right now.

Action(Values-based prioritization) **+** *Community* **+** *Self-care* **=** *Having It All*

It really is that simple. The secret sauce to maintaining this 'Having It All' lifestyle is to repeat the equation when you enter a new season of your life or—said the mathematically correct way—the variables within your 'Have It All' life equation change. The act of consistently checking in with your priorities allows you to make minor adjustments as needed instead of a complete overhaul as you uncomfortably head into a new and different season of your life. All seasons of your life will bring unique challenges that will cause your priorities to shift. The gift you can give yourself is listening and being in tune with those changes so you can be proactive in how you go about shifting the pieces of your puzzle to create a better overall picture.

It's like playing Tetris, except the multicolored blocks in this version of the game that need to fit together are different aspects of your life. Or as Jean Thompson, the CEO of Seattle Chocolates, likes to think of it—a well-balanced diet.

TIMING IS EVERYTHING

Jean and I discussed the common pushback to the idea of Having It All. Her initial reaction to the phrase wasn't disdain or fear or panic. Jean believes that one can modify the statement and then the impossible becomes possible. "Yes, I believe you can Have It All—just not all at the exact same time."

Jean suggests the staggered approach. "We don't eat every single meal perfectly nutritionally, or at least I don't. But over the course of the day, I have a balanced diet. I need a whole day to kind of fit it all in."

Have you ever had waffles drizzled with melted butter and smothered with maple syrup with a side of bacon for breakfast? What did you eat for the rest of the day? Did you maybe have some fruit and a green salad for lunch? What about dinner? Was it one of a million ways to cook chicken and veggies? Just because you had a sugar high at the beginning of your day doesn't mean that you had Haagen-Dazs coffee ice cream for lunch and a massive piece of Pie Bar's strawberry rhubarb pie with its wonderfully delicious matching cocktail for dinner.

MATH ISN'T FLEXIBLE/TIME STOPS FOR NO WOMAN

Life is the same way. In a new season, there are new priorities and therefore new elements of life to take into consideration. If you want to indulge your sweet tooth or, in this case, pursue a new goal, you have to balance that new element with the rest of the priorities in your life. Jean believes, "I need my whole life to fit in all the things that I want to do. You can't do it all at the same time. There are only so many hours in the day."

There are only twenty-four hours in a day. Cold. Hard. Truth. No matter how many times I try to redo the math and get creative with my order of operations, the day only breaks down one way. Allot your time carefully, strategically, and compassionately.

TIME-MANAGING WOMEN

I want to direct your attention to thirty women who are systematically designing and redesigning their lives to fit with their priorities in their current season of their lives. Within these pages are incredible women. I want to call them ordinary so that everyone feels like they can relate to them, but I can't bring myself to reduce the individuality of these special women.

On the contrary, there are so many diverse women in this book—each at different phases in their lives, with different backgrounds, in different industries, with different belief systems and different goals—that you may not personally resonate with all of them on a piecemeal level. If you pay close attention to their path, however, the universal truths these women portray to the rest of us are real and inspiring.

A NEW MODEL

POWER AND FAILURE

With this new definition of what Having It All means, it flips the model. What sets these women, who live their lives in this designed way, apart is that they understand on some level how powerful they can be. Whether it is the strength of their characters or their epic brain power or their physical athletic capabilities, these women understand they are a force to be reckoned with. Part of their power lies in the fact that they are human. They make mistakes and have the ability to learn and grow from their experiences. One of my favorite themes to broach with all those I interviewed was failure!

RESILIENCE

This leads me to the next quality that bonds the women in these pages—resilience. I can't even begin to adequately describe how diverse the circumstances that have built these women are. Valerie Palmer grew up in South Africa during Apartheid as a mixed-race woman and is adamant that her formative experience in that environment unlocked her success later in life. Through miscarriages, divorce, moves across the country, and loss of jobs, these women have honed their resilience, created through struggle mixed with a pinch of defiance. The result is a refusal to be kept down and out or in whatever situation has beaten them to the place where they can only move up.

CHOICE

Finally, they are united in choice. These women actively chose to pursue the life they hoped to live at each fork in their individual roads, which led them where they are today. Life will throw you punches and curveballs. You can either duck or swing or let both hit you. Any way you slice it or any approach you take—active or passive—there is still power in your choice and agency when you decide to actively take the reins. A woman we will call Jane chose to leave her husband when his actions landed their family in financial ruin. As a Wealth Management

Advisor, she was trained to know when to cut her losses and invest elsewhere. She actively chose to save herself and her daughter.

That being said, here are three truths to keep in mind while reading this book:

Truth One: There are Different Seasons in Life

When I say "different seasons," what I mean is a new phase of your life requiring you to reprioritize the things on your Personal Value List. Your Personal Value List consists of the elements in your life that you deem most important. For some, this may be the three F's: Family, Faith, Friends. For others, the list may be made up of a combination of Physical and Mental Health, Work, or Volunteering. It depends on you as an individual and what you find gives you the most return on your investment in that area of your life.

When you restructure this list in new seasons of your life, often new elements swoop in and displace previous ones. For example, if you are in the New Mom Season of your life, does self-care get bumped off the list? Be honest with yourself! Each new season requires you to be flexible, adaptable, and open to change. Your *resilience* teaches you how to do these things.

When you're going through different stages, feeling lost is easy. One way to find guidance through all of the chaos is to have a Personal Board of Directors. These are people you select for various reasons to act as mentors, a sounding board, or whatever you need in that season of your life. By having these people in your corner, rooting for your success, it is proven that you will be more confident as you navigate the turbulent seasons of life and less afraid to take a new path, if you choose. For more on creating your Personal Board of Directors, check out Shannon Vetto's story in Chapter 5: Growing Your Community.

As you move through the seasons of your life, you change with them. Every time you read this book, you'll be a different person, so you'll get something different out of it.

"You never step in the same river twice." — Heraclitus[1].

Every time you pick up this book, you'll be in a different season and different messages will resonate with you—so let these stories work as one of the members of your Board of Directors—these stories are collected for your benefit to use over time as you find different ones apply.

---

1   Graham, Daniel W., "Heraclitus", *The Stanford Encyclopedia of Philosophy* (Fall 2019 Edition), Edward N. Zalta (ed.),

Truth Two: There Is Strength in Numbers

You are not an island. Don't act like asking for help is an admission that you are less than who you are. It takes great strength to lean on your community. You have to make the *choice* to let your people help you toward whatever dream or goal or load of laundry you are trying to fold and put away.

You are not alone. Other people are interested in seeing you shine and live your dreams. Connect with them. Create your community.

Community is created through being vulnerable. It is necessary to put yourself out there to reap the benefits of the kind of supportive closeness that comes with relationship building. Some ways to go about building out your community that are demonstrated through these stories are partnership, mentorship, friendship, and family.

You will find instances of sacrifice and how those experiences shaped and reframed personal and professional lives. In some cases, the sacrifices made involved giving up some of the people who were no longer serving a positive purpose in their lives. As a training triathlete, Kalee Tyson had to give up some of her 'party' friends to pursue the lifestyle she wanted to live. She couldn't go to happy hour every week and be as social as she used to be prior to embarking on her Iron Man journey. For Kalee, what is important right now isn't the large number of friendships, it's the fewer friends at higher quality who respect her vision and goals.

When one has to make the choice to sacrifice something important to them, it helps when you have a shoulder to lean on, propping you up as you make it.

Your Tribe is Not Your Life

Creating a tribe involves all sorts of challenges. Again, there are only twenty-four hours in the day. How does one juggle a job and a personal life? The popularized term work-life balance has been played out and disproven many times over. There are also other theories riffing off the term. Amazon dubbed this blending of work and personal life Work-Life Harmony. Others in the tech industry have called it Work-Life Integration. Some believe it to be impossible! That there is perpetual imbalance and that all the elements in your life can never be in perfect harmony at the exact same time. Guess what? They are right! These are buzzwords founded in the idea that as an individual you need to divide your time equally amongst all the different aspects of your life. The result? Spreading yourself too thin.

This may sound ridiculous but think of your life like a piece of toast. I love toast with Kerry Gold Irish butter and strawberry jam. The sweet and salty pairing creates the perfect flavor profile for my palate. Think about what you love to put on your toast. My Nana taught me to spread my jam all the way out to the crust of my bread, creating a thin delicious layer to be savored with each bite. My dad, however, is a gobs-of-jam-at-the-center-of-the-toast kind of guy. He does not evenly distribute, and that works just fine for him. We all spread our jam in different ways and in different proportions. Experiment and find out which allocation of whatever happens to be your JAM is the best for your personal happiness and roll with it. Use the technique of these women as guideposts for figuring out what works best in your life.

Another interesting look into community formation is the preexisting institutional lack-thereof. Women in male-dominated industries tell their stories to illuminate how they navigate their professional worlds to find success. It is easy to default into 'being one of the guys' in these situations. Women like Gillian Crismier share how they were able to use their powerful feminine instincts to unlock success in their careers. I'm talking supersonic mom-strength, empathy, next-level multi-tasking and active listening in action.

Truth Three: Don't Allow Yourself to Sacrifice Your Passion

There is power in pursuing your passion. You are important. Put yourself on your priority list. You are the only person living your life. Living it fully—whatever that means as defined by you—should be your sole aim. To live your life in this way, it is absolutely necessary to make yourself a priority. Put yourself in front of other people's wants and desires. Don't let anyone or anything be a detriment to your goals or a hindrance in achieving your dream. By allowing them to invade that most private part of your life, you give them too much power. This statement is especially true if you're putting someone else above or before yourself.

You may be saying to yourself right now, "But I am a Mom. This doesn't apply to me!" This especially applies to you. In her book, *Girl, Wash Your Face*[2], Rachel Hollis spells this out loud and clear. If you are not functioning at peak performance by taking care of yourself—physically, mentally, emotionally—then you will not be able to show up for your kids in the way that they need you to. It is a simple idea but not easy to put into practice.

---

2   Hollis, Rachel. *Girl, Wash Your Face*. Nelson Books, 2018.

Enter the idea of Controlled Selfishness. It's okay to be Number One in your own book. Don't let other people dictate how you should spend your time. When you're looking back on your life in your old age, the only person who feels the weight of regret from the things you didn't do or didn't reach for or didn't try out is yourself. Nobody else is going to carry that burden for you. What are you willing to regret when you look back and what are you not willing to give up?

Use your power to pursue your passion. Who knows, you could be like Chelsey White and turn your passion into your paycheck! Walking away from a stable job as a Financial Analyst at L'Oréal was not easy for Chelsey. She had a fiancé and their Manhattan rent to think of when she quit and took her company Chelsweets full time as an Instagram cake-baking and decorating influencer! Find out more about how other women used their power to live out their dreams as we discuss their passion projects.

Just behind the curtain of every success sits hundreds of failures. I can say confidently every single woman in this book has experienced failure. It freaking stings worse than pouring hydrogen peroxide on an open wound. The test of your power comes in how you perceive and respond to failure. By taking ownership of your failure, analyzing your missteps and circumstances surrounding the situation, and trying again, you need to understand that you really haven't failed at all. If you ruminate on the negative and let the fear of what other people will think of your failure prevent you from trying again, then you will never experience success.

True success is learned. You have to build that muscle up through failing over and over and over again until you are equipped enough to handle the project, dream, or goal you are attempting to tackle. If you are reading this and thinking, "Wow, I've never failed at anything in my life before... this doesn't apply to me!" then, girlfriend, you are not dreaming big enough.

Success is also hard-earned. So many women do not pause to appreciate how they got to where they are. Many never feel like they have arrived at the level of success they hope to achieve. It is important to take stock of your accomplishments and appreciate what incredible things you as an individual are able to accomplish.

Pro Tip: Write them all down. When you are having a bad day, go back to this list and let yourself acknowledge your accomplishments to interrupt whenever horribly negative talk-track is running through your head. Mental health is just as important as physical health. Self-care is quite possibly my favorite topic in this book, partly because I was shocked to learn through interviews how many incredible women don't practice it.

Read on to discover what self-care means to women in all different walks of life. Learn from the mistakes of other women who didn't prioritize it early enough in their careers or who let it fall off their priority list when they became mothers. Whether it is physical activity, mindfulness, or a Mommy Play Date to get you out of the house, it is important that you use these women's stories to help define what self-care means to you. For Caroline Reis, it means meditation as she commutes to and from work on the ferry. What will it mean for you?

MOMS! Wow, you are about to get so much great insight into how women have been able to pursue their careers while raising awesome children. You will also hear stories from incredible women who were successful in their careers and chose to stay at home with their children. There is no right way to be a mom. Let me say that again for the ladies in the back rolling their eyes.

THERE IS NO RIGHT WAY TO BE A MOTHER TO YOUR CHILDREN.

All you can do is your best and show them the type of person you are authentically so that they understand what is important to you in life.

These three truths we will hold self-evident. Each story—just like each woman—is unique, special, and all her own.

Read on. These women are rad!

Chapter 2

Kids First, Then Career

Who wins the race in the old wives' tale about the tortoise and the hare? Keep that in mind as you read the following stories of three absolutely incredible women with very different approaches to life, parenting, and work.

JEAN THE CHOCOLATE QUEEN

Meet Jean Thompson. Mother and CEO of Seattle Chocolate.

According to a review done by researchers at the University of Michigan, Jean is an anomaly. In their research, two cultural anthologists found that the cultural narrative portrayed women in stereotypical and static roles.

They found that "women are socially constructed as either mothers or workers, *but not both.*[3]"

We live in an 'either/or' society. The options are either white chocolate or dark chocolate. Milk chocolate isn't even on the table.

Time to break out of that restrictive, prescriptive mentality society has forced upon you whether you actively know it or not. Girls have been taught for centuries the "types" of women that exist in the world. From the mothers to the working women and all the variations in between, social stigma and biases restrict us from daring to dream.

When you shed this limited mindset, you are capable of building any life you want to live —layering on motherhood and interweaving a career as you see fit. It is never too late to reconfigure your thinking. Just break it down into terms that are more digestible.

If someone had asked Jean to speculate how her life would unfold, she never would have predicted the full, ever-evolving life she has built for herself today. Her

---

3   Paré, Elizabeth and Heather Dillway. ""Staying at Home" versus "Working": A Call for Broader Conceptualizations of Parenthood and Paid Work." *Michigan Family Review*, no. 10(2005): 66-87.

circumstances have shifted in each new season of her life, giving her many data points to pull from as she formulated her unique perspective on life and women supporting other women.

In her experience, Having It All is much like eating a balanced diet—intentional and achievable over time.

THE BALANCED DIET APPROACH

"We don't eat every single meal perfectly nutritionally— or at least I don't." Jean laughed. "But over the course of the day, I have a balanced diet. I need a whole day to fit it all in. So in much the same way, I need my whole lifetime to fit in all the things I want to do. No one can do it all at the same time. There are only so many hours in a day."

Striving to achieve a life equally divided amongst your priorities every single day is setting yourself up for failure. Yes, this is where time management, prioritization, and trust in your own abilities will take you lightyears ahead of the rest of humankind. Still, all of those planning and organizational components only get you so far. Life throws you curveballs.

Jean believes she brings a unique perspective to the table.

She has lived so many different seasons of her life that have informed her outlook. Looking at the world in black and white wasn't going to cut it where Jean was concerned. Looking at life through that 'either/or' lens didn't suffice to convey her whole experience. In chronological order, Jean has lived her life as:

- A single, working woman
- A married woman working at Microsoft
- A married woman working from home
- A married mom volunteering in the community
- A married working mom as CEO of Seattle Chocolate
- A single working mom as CEO of Seattle Chocolate
- A re-married, working mom as CEO of Seattle Chocolate

She managed to experience all of the different possible life combinations—a very rare accomplishment. Jean was honest with herself and introspective about what she needed in each season of her life, and she led with those concepts in her decision making.

Jean is refreshingly candid when talking about her life's curvy path, "I've done all of those things. They are all possible, and they are all rewarding in their own way. None is worse than the other. It really is what you choose and that is the most empowering thing about being a woman. Women have this choice." She did qualify that men and women alike have this sense of choice. Yet she really felt women are specifically empowered by their ability to choose their path at any given point in their lives.

There are moments that beg for choice.

Jean described her life as a young working mother. She worked sixty hours a week at Microsoft. She was all in all the time. Yet, when she started having kids, a switch flipped in her brain and everything seemed so trivial in comparison to being a mother. Following that 'aha' moment, Jean decided to quit Microsoft and stay at home. It was her choice. At the time, the most important thing to her was raising her children.

"Most people kind of make a choice early on in their lives to pursue a career, be a working mom, or decide to stay at home." Jean describes how often that each type of woman listed above tends to put down—whether out loud or in their own head—the choices of the other two types of women because they have this impulse to substantiate the choice they personally made. She's heard all of the extreme statements people attach to other's life choices, "Either people are very ambitious or they don't care that much about their career or they don't love their kids as much." Jean expressed a deep-rooted sense of frustration that women feel the need to tear other women down just to justify their personal choices. Fortunately, she noted this type of dialogue seems to be changing slowly but surely.

We all have the ability to make choices. To truly empower one another as women, Jean believes whole-heartedly, "We need to stop trashing each other's choices." When we can accomplish that feat, collective and individual success will exponentially increase.

THE BENEFIT OF NATURAL DISASTERS

When Jean's youngest went to kindergarten, it was time for her to think about how she wanted to spend her time. She was afraid of being terribly bored with all of the kids out of the house. Her love of kids actually got her thinking she might want to get a teaching certificate. "I loved hanging out with kids—all kids, not just my own. They crack me up, I could watch them all day!" She tentatively put a plan in place to start down the track of becoming a teacher.

Life had different plans for her! "You kind of feel your way and decide what works for you at that time, and if you are lucky enough to have an opportunity, you have to grab it." That is exactly what happened when the 2001 earthquake rocked Seattle. What was scary and devasting for the community as a whole brought a unique opportunity into Jean's life that would change it for the better, although she didn't know that then.

She and her husband were investors in the company Seattle Chocolate. The earthquake left the factory in ruins. Someone needed to step up financially, so she and her husband contributed. Who doesn't love chocolate, right? In helping right Seattle Chocolate, Jean and her husband became the majority owners of the company. It was a difficult time and even a year later, they were still struggling to make payroll.

At that point, Jean decided to forgo the idea of becoming a teacher and devote twenty hours a week to help the sales and marketing side of the business. Her daughter was in kindergarten at the time, so it made sense for her to occupy herself with a part-time role. After working at Microsoft as a Corporate Communications Manager, marketing the product was in her wheelhouse. Jean even opted out of taking a paycheck. She truly wanted to volunteer her time to keep Seattle Chocolate afloat.

Just when the situation couldn't get any bleaker, the CEO quit. They didn't have the money to bring in anyone new. The only other option was to let the company go out of business, in which case, thirty people would lose their jobs and her personal investment in Seattle Chocolate would melt away.

When Jean was approached to take on the role of CEO, she rejected the idea. At the time, she genuinely believed she didn't even really like business. However, when it came down to taking the job or letting the company go under, she couldn't let that happen. Jean recalls her not-so-positive approach to her new role, "Well, I'm better than nothing. That was the kind of mindset I had to have going into this thing to get me to do it."

FAILING FORWARD

It was trial by fire over and over and over again until she figured out what worked.

Jean looks back at her whirlwind start as CEO with humorous disbelief. She had never stepped foot into a manufacturing facility before the one that she was destined to run just six weeks later. "That was it. That was all the time I had to learn how to be a CEO. Prior to that, I really only had been in Costco's warehouse, and I'm not sure that helped at all!"

With Costco as her guide, Jean was off to the races getting a crash course in supply chain management. "I didn't know anything about that whole operation side of the business. I had never run a company; I didn't know how to even read a financial statement!" said Jean, making sure to emphasize, "I. Was. A. Marketer." Her perceived lack of preparedness worked in her favor. "Luckily, I didn't know very much so I didn't realize how foolish it was for me to try to take this on. Ignorance was bliss in my case."

Jean enthusiastically put on the hat of entrepreneur and used her optimism to her advantage. "Really, how hard can it be? Chocolate is something I love. It was a consumer product, and there was a tremendous amount of packaging and marketing that went into it." She learned on the fly and planned her next move by the week then by the month and by the year when she was able to afford that luxury.

When everything is brand-spanking new, every situation you encounter is a learning moment. The amount of personal growth that happens in such a condensed period of time can be astonishing. Looking back on her seventeen years as the CEO of Seattle Chocolate, Jean was surprised at the personal development she experienced. "What surprised me the most is how patient I've been, because it really wasn't in my nature at all." Jean previously would find herself bored three to four years into a role and then move on to the next adventure. This routine happened consistently in her life until she landed at Seattle Chocolate.

It took more than half a decade to even feel like she truly deserved to be acting as CEO for the company. "I think I felt like for the first five years, I was a total imposter. I had no idea what I was doing." This concept of imposter syndrome prevents so many women from actually reaching for jobs that they really want for fear of lack of experience. Jean kept qualifying who she was and what she did because she felt she didn't have the experience to back it up. "I keep saying I'm an entrepreneur, but I'm really not. I kept saying I'm the CEO but really not." After the five-year mark. she felt she'd earned the right to own her role. "I haven't arrived but I am along the spectrum of getting to where I want to be."

Did you know that on average men will apply for jobs they are only sixty percent qualified for whereas women will only for jobs they are one hundred percent qualified for? This is outrageous. If there is a program you don't know how to use, more often than not, you can learn it on the job. It's a cheesy concept but when you shoot for the moon, you absolutely will land amongst the stars. Men do it. Ladies, time to reframe how we evaluate job descriptions!

Jean feels like she got lucky. The company's situation was improving, and she was learning what worked through trial and error. "I was developing a huge database of what not to do." Since aggregating her What-Not-To-Do Data, Jean uses it to guide her in the right direction.

She now demands the respect she deserves in the role. Not in an obnoxious way. When she runs across the occasional situation where she is not treated with the respect she deserves, Jean confidently and powerfully realigns expectations of the person she is dealing with. Her tone, confidence, and power are difficult to ignore.

Jean's trust in her own ability to continually learn and grow is her secret weapon. It is what has informed the difficult decisions she has made in each new season of her life. Her experiences over time have allowed her to experience all of the things that are important on her priority list.

LIFE ISN'T ALL DESSERT ALL THE TIME
The evolution of Jean's life did not come without consequences. Two big sacrifices come to mind when she thinks about what she has missed in living her life the way she has designed it.

The first is that Jean feels she missed out on spending more time with her son. When Jean went back to work as the CEO of Seattle Chocolate, her son was twelve. She didn't realize how her career had impacted her son until she was sitting around the dinner table one night right before he graduated high school. Around the table sat Jean, his father, and his girlfriend.

Intermixed among casual dinner conversation, her son's girlfriend asked Jean how many hours a week she usually worked. Before she could answer, her son chimed in saying, "Oh, she works constantly. She doesn't get home until almost eight o'clock at night." She was shocked. Jean knew she didn't burn the candle until eight every night. In reality, what her son meant was this—she was never around. It didn't matter what time she literally got home. The feeling stuck with Jean. She does regret sacrificing some of the quality time she could have spent with her son.

The second sacrifice that comes to mind was her potential momentum in the workforce if she had not stayed at home for ten years with her kids. Ten years is a long time to be out of the game. "I would be ten years farther ahead. In my case, it doesn't really matter because I own my own business. But if you were trying to compete in the *Fortune 500* world then it would have cost you.

It would be hard to catch up." Being out of the work-force for ten years equates to a significant loss in earning power as well as the confidence one gains through tenured experience. That confidence is the X-factor in rising above the rest.

An incredible amount of confidence can be built by having a consistent source from which you can measure your growth or contribution. When stay-at-home moms transition back into the workforce or even those who are contemplating making the move back into the professional world, Jean has seen the lack of confidence perpetuate negative self-beliefs. "I've seen that with my peers who stay at home. They feel they don't have much to offer when they're applying for a job. That just is not true. They absolutely have something to offer. They've done the hardest job out there. They'll learn quickly!"

IT TAKES A VILLAGE TO RAISE A BUSINESS

You don't get there alone. Growing—whether it be as a mother or as a businesswoman—requires some outside influence. Jean found a nationwide entrepreneurial organization that has influenced her on both a professional and personal level. "What's fun is being fifty-eight years old, still running a company, and hanging with people in this business community who are in their thirties and forties. Some may be in their fifties, but I'm one of the oldest by far. It's such a treat. I feel younger and more vibrant, and there is so much of my life ahead of me because of these people." The gender breakdown of the group is nowhere close to even. Jean thinks it is comprised of eighty-five percent men nationwide. However, the women have a unique opportunity to voice their opinions and beliefs in a way their peers will hear.

In her vibrant business community, the concept of work-life balance came up as a topic of discussion. Jean saw that both men and women struggle with the idea. However, in her opinion, the women in the room had it figured out better than the men! "Of course, there were only two of us, so I'm not sure that can be representational of all women." Jean was quick to qualify her statement yet had legitimate reasoning to stand by her theory.

This shocked me. From the interviews I've conducted, I was under the impression that women have an extremely difficult time creating a feeling of stability between work and personal life. Her answer was so simple I couldn't believe I hadn't thought of it myself. "As women, we have the great gift of the maternal instinct. So for me, the balance was always between family and work. It was never even a question for the two women in the group what was at the top of our priority list. For the men, it was harder, because they were concerned about their reputation. Didn't want to be seen as a slouch or not dedicated to their jobs." For Jean, it was never a question. Everything else will always take a backseat to her family. "If my kids needed me, I was there! I never felt guilty about having to leave work."

To her surprise, Jean also never felt guilty about leaving her kids. "After spending ten straight years at home with my kids, I thought I would feel some guilt going back to work. But I never felt guilty. I think they liked having some independence from me. Instead of being with me every minute, they had time to spend with other people who were influential in their lives, more time with friends, more time alone to just think and figure things out for themselves, which has benefited them." Today, her children are extremely independent people. Jean is so proud her son went to live in Tokyo, pursuing his interests with reckless abandon and has now returned home to pursue a career in high tech. Her daughter just graduated from college in 2019 and started working at Seattle Chocolate with the hope to one day take over the business. Being a strong savvy woman must run in the family!

Jean is not slowing down. At fifty-eight, she has set new audacious goals for herself. She wants to travel to seventy countries by the age of seventy! From memory, she can come up with forty-four countries spanning all corners of the world that she has visited to date—only twenty-three more to go! She also has a wonderful travel partner to do it with! Five years ago, Jean married a wonderful man who gave up his career as an aerospace engineer to support her and her company. Jean is lucky to have travel tied into her role as CEO of Seattle Chocolate. She is able to explore interesting places in Central and South America as well as several West African countries where cacao is grown. She hopes to pass the baton to her daughter around that birthday milestone as well.

Jean's strength and drive are awe-inspiring. Her final words of advice to me were, "Listen, you get to design your life and nobody gets to tell you what to do or put limits on what you want to achieve." The emphatic emotion behind her words motivated me to take a hard look at my goals and what I want to accomplish. I hope her story does the same for you.

P.S. as I wrote this story, two women-led companies were valued at $1 billion this week—Spanx and Rent-the-Runway. Who knows! Your own venture could be next.

GO YOUR OWN PACE LIKE
NANCY OUTCALT

Jean is right; you are the only person who gets to put limits on your life. You are the only decision-maker who counts when it comes to designing the life you want for YOU.

Sometimes, those decisions require a leap of faith...

HEADFIRST INTO THE DEEP END

Nancy Outcalt was working on a cruise ship when she met her future husband, Rob. The two sailed around for almost a year on the same ship, falling in love. At the end of that year, he asked her to move to Seattle with him. She had three things to consider when faced with a huge life decision:

1. The guy—Nancy *loved* him and seriously thought he was the one for her. Plus, who wouldn't fall in love sailing around the world for a year? Best courtSHIP!
2. The location—Seattle. A city clear across the country from where she grew up in Chicago. It was never before visited, uncharted territory far away from all of Nancy's friends and family.
3. Professional prospects—She didn't have a job. Prior to working on the cruise ship, Nancy was in

advertising. She had professional experience but she hadn't actively checked out the job market in advance of moving there.

Nancy chose to take the gigantic leap of faith and pivot from her advertising career into IT training services at Training Access. Nancy is an excellent pulse-checker. She was the one who could be dragged and dropped in different customer companies to evaluate and consult on personalized training for employees. She was brought on in a consulting capacity at CompuCom to determine whether incorporating training services into their product portfolio would be a lucrative business strategy.

After a three-month evaluation, Nancy came to the conclusion that would put her out of a job. The company should not—in her professional opinion—incorporate the services she was able to provide.

As a result of her candor, the company recognized her talent and integrity and decided to shift her into another part of the organization. A connector by nature, Nancy found herself recruiting executive leadership and was extremely successful in attracting quality talent.

PIVOT, ADJUST, REPEAT

Around that same time, she married the man she moved to Seattle for and was having her first child. Her priorities were shifting due to her adventure into motherhood and she needed to restructure her professional life. Nancy brought a plan to her management team proposing that she work four days a week for ten hours a day. This change still offered the company a total of forty hours a week and afforded her the luxury of an extra day at home with her daughter. When she was at work, a few other moms at the office recommended the cutest and most qualified at-home daycare for her to use. At lunch, Nancy was able to run over and breastfeed her daughter; it was the picture of convenience. The arrangement worked well for about seventeen months, but then she had her next child.

Unfortunately, the daycare she loved closed and so she had to change the way she operated for baby number two. Nancy hired a nanny. At this point, CompuCom went digital, allowing her to work at home. As a young mom, it was almost unbearable. Nancy described the early days of working from home, "It was so hard to hear my kids crying. I had to just hold myself up in my office and try not to go out and comfort them. It was really disruptive for me, as well as for my kids." She cut her hours further to thirty-two in order to spend as much time as possible with her kids while still maintaining full benefits.

In 2000, just before the .com boom and bust, a bright and shiny opportunity presented itself at a cool startup. To convince her to leave the flexibility and security she felt with CompuCom, this startup offered her a fifty-percent salary increase, the potential to earn a BMW, and complete autonomy over her schedule. They said all the right things, and Nancy was convinced to move right on over. After a short time working at the startup, the illusion was shattered. All those promises had been empty. Nancy found herself working twice as many hours and, worst of all, missing out on time with her kids. In her own words, "It was horrible, and I was so unbelievably stressed out." To illustrate how this professional pressure was manifesting in her personal life, Nancy confided a story that completely changed the way she prioritized her life.

THE SHOCK FACTOR

During her second daughter's well-baby visit, the doctor asked Nancy if she was worried. Nancy was confused by what the doctor meant. What was there to be concerned about?

The doctor earnestly pointed Nancy's attention to a fact that hadn't even registered on her radar of importance. "Aren't you worried she isn't speaking yet?"

Nancy was in shock. She stuttered in reply, "I-I hadn't noticed." As she recounted this experience, emotion charged Nancy's voice. In that moment, she was not the type of mom she wanted to be. Thankfully, that well-baby visit put her priorities in razor-sharp focus. Nancy set to work on reorganizing her priority list. Nancy immediately called the top five child language specialists on the east side. After thorough evaluations, it was determined her daughter was fine and in time, it was clear she just had a quiet nature.

I am a firm believer that everything happens for a reason. When the .com bubble burst the startup blew through all of its venture capital. Money being tight, the recruiting team at the company faced a harsh reality. There were eleven recruiters and the company could only afford to keep one. Nancy, being the most recent hire on the team, was laid off. She could not have been more ecstatic to leave that hot-mess of a situation.

SAVE YOURSELF

Savvy as she is, Nancy came up with an incredible Plan B. She founded her own recruiting company, A-List Recruiting. Get this—Nancy's first customer was the company that had just laid her off! There has to be some awesome karmic energy behind that. They still needed to bring people in, and they found a way to use Nancy's talents by paying her out of a separate budget. By all accounts, her lifestyle shouldn't have changed dramatically. However, this time, she was able to set the limits and boundaries necessary to be the mom she wanted to be while still fulfilling her core desire to connect individuals with amazing opportunities.

In the ten years of success Nancy had with A-List Recruiting, she was able to be PTA President, volunteer in her daughter's classrooms, help—on a pro bono basis—friends (and their kids) enhance their resumes, and chaperone every single volleyball tournament her daughter played in. Nancy found a way to contribute to a Seattle Children's Hospital Guild close to her heart in the form of acting president, auction chair, and more, as well as gather monthly with five girlfriends spending quality time together through their Gourmet Club. She was both personally and professionally fulfilled in that season of her life.

As her girls entered high school, they did not need (or want) her around as often. With this new development, Nancy found running her own business isolating. She missed the camaraderie in an office and the energy in bouncing ideas off of coworkers. Nancy happened to grab lunch with her ex-boss at CompuCom. By dessert, she offered Nancy an opportunity to pick up right where she left off within the organization—doing what she loved!

Today, Nancy has pivoted into a sales role essentially selling the value of her recruiting services. In this new phase of her life, Nancy has one goal: kick her career into high gear. When I asked her what that looked like, Nancy said, "I want to make the investment in myself and help others to be successful and, of course, the commensurate compensation. I don't feel like I need to manage a team; I already manage a family and kids." With her drive and dedication, Nancy has accomplished incredible feats in her new role later in her career. She is reclaiming time for herself and dedicating that time to achieving the lofty personal goals she has set forth. This woman can accomplish anything—and she has—all at her own pace!

JENN LEITCH KNOWS IT IS NEVER TOO LATE TO LEARN MORE

Never say never.

Jenn Leitch got her Associate Degree in Nursing at a local community college and started her career as a bedside nurse at just twenty-one years old. She came from a modest, lower-income household and knew she if she wanted to go to school she was going to have to make it happen for herself. "I was putting myself through school. So when I got out, I had to work to pay the bills. At that time, I couldn't afford the luxury of stopping work to go back and finish my degree." Initially, Jenn studied nursing to get into the Peace Corps. Little did she know that she would find herself twenty years down the road managing a division of the hospital she didn't even know existed!

How did she get there? One giant push from someone who saw her potential.

FROM UNDERDOG TO TOPDOG

In the nursing profession, education is everything. To paint a picture of the competitive environment, Jenn remarked, "Master's degrees are like high school diplomas. It's just a piece of paper you have to have in nursing." With such an emphasis on degrees, education, and certifications, Jenn felt like an underdog coming in with her Associate's level education. She spent the next nine years perfecting her craft, consuming and learning everything she could about bedside nursing in the neurosurgery/trauma unit.

If you ask Jenn, she will self-identify as one who shoots for the moon. "I've always had big dreams." Yet it took a push from someone who knew her work ethic to get the ball rolling on achieving those big dreams. One of Jenn's managers approached her and challenged her to go back to school. At that point, she had been out of the classroom for at least fifteen years. When she started looking into completing her Bachelor's degree, it was an overwhelming process but she settled on an online program as that's what fit best for her family. To top it off, she also had a one-year-old and a three-year-old at home to worry about while she made the decision to go back to school—no easy task to manage.

Even an online degree program was a little intimidating at first for Jenn. "I took statistics online, and there wasn't even a calculator anymore! But I got through. I just kept going." When you are overwhelmed or daunted by the task in front of you, return to the overarching purpose behind what you are doing. It can provide just the healthy dose of perspective you need to keep on grinding through until the end. Remember it is okay to get overwhelmed and cry it out! In Jenn's case, much of the tear wiping was done by her husband; her best friend, cheerleader, buffer, and insecurity-crusher.

Her perseverance was rewarded! The term before she was done with her degree, that same mentor approached Jenn and offered her a huge promotion—that mentor's very own job managing the nurses. "I just about passed out. It was my first week back at work; I had been on a leave of absence because my father passed away. I definitely was not in the frame of mind to fill anyone's shoes." Her mentor insisted that Jenn was the only person she could entrust her beloved team to. That woman wouldn't take no for an answer! "She said she couldn't leave the organization unless she knew it was in good hands, and then chose me to be Interim. I was truly shocked." The underdog got her shot! Her decision to go back to school was the catalyst for a chain reaction of personal and professional growth that has kept her career climbing at a steady pace.

As her career flourished, Jenn was invited to speak at a national nurse's executive conference. Although she had earned her moment in the spotlight, she came down with a terrible case of imposter syndrome. She called her husband in pure terror the night before. "I can't do this, who the hell do I think I am? These are executives with PhDs and I'm a poor girl from Aloha."

He answered, "Maybe, but they want to hear what YOU have to say! You're the poo, honey, take a whiff." The bad quote from a '90s cheerleader movie made her smile and calmed her nerves. Even when her confidence wavered,

Jenn has the support system in place to lift her up and help her keep going!

Down the road, Jenn asked that mentor why she gave her a shot. Jenn's former director told her she saw her "light." Jenn's passion for her work, commitment to education and personal improvement, as well as her unwavering drive were what earned her the incredible opportunities both big and small. One of the bigger ones was the chance to speak at the C-level with her boss on a weekly basis. Jenn's "light" and the influence of that mentor pushed her to put her hand up for new and exciting opportunities, such as building out roles within the Nurse Care Management Organization at one of the top leading academic medical centers in the nation. In her role now, as Nurse Care Manager of the Care Management Division, Jenn makes a point to recognize the "light" within those who work for her to nurture their own learning and growth.

MAKING SCHOOL LOOK COOL

The encouragement Jenn received from trusted mentors was just one piece of the puzzle to building her success. In order to be present with her family, run her organization, and go back to school a second time to earn her Master's, Jenn took a hard look at her priorities.

On the top of the list was family. Jenn and her husband decided that both of their careers were extremely important to them but family would be put above all else. Although she and her husband are on the same page, not everyone she worked with could understand her choice and one specific incident has stuck with her as a working mom.

Upon returning from a week-long vacation with her family, Jenn was in a meeting with important C-level officers. After some small talk at the beginning of the meeting about her vacation, the Chief Medical Officer turned to her and said, "Oh, your kids are probably so sad to see you go back to work. They must miss their mommy!" His comment is the perfect example of what not to say to a working mom.

Jenn immediately corrected the CMO's thinking by saying, "Actually, my kids are really excited to go back to preschool. It is where they thrive!"

Jenn has worked too hard to create a learning environment for her children to have it be diminished by one comment. She believes that every child's "normal" is different and predicated on the environment in which they were raised. Her kids grew up going to preschool and were not only used to it as a part of their routine, they loved it! She is convinced that if she all-of-a-sudden started to stay at home with them all day, every day they wouldn't know how to operate. Regardless, her choice works for her family and that is not to be judged by anyone else with another idea of what the role of "Mommy" should look like. Her kids have seen Jenn go back to school not once but twice and quite frankly have a badass example role-modeling for them just how cool learning can be. Why wouldn't they love going to preschool and acquire new knowledge?

With so many different pieces to the puzzle that is Jenn's life, it is an epic game of Tetris trying to figure out how to make them all fit together. "As bad as it sounds, I even have to schedule time to be spontaneous." Jenn remains hyper-organized in order to function at the levels she wants to in the different areas of her life. It actually becomes a stressor for Jenn when her schedule isn't built out. "I don't live in last-minute-land. I really hate those people who can leave everything to the very last minute and still get it done. I just don't operate that way." By structuring a definitive schedule, Jenn is able to create space for self-care. As she completes her Master's, Jenn rearranged her work schedule to consist of a four-day week working ten hours per day. This way, on her day off, Jenn can cram a meager sixteen hours of school work into one day. Talk about calendar chess!

Jenn loves spending time with her children. They are only seven and nine once! Jenn and her husband make a concerted effort to make sure the time they have to spend together is high-quality and uninterrupted. "I'm in the thick of it. Really, we like to do a lot of family outings and trips and just spending a lot one-on-one time, which is so precious. If I was not highly organized with school as a full-time job and running an entire organization, school and work would just scope-creep on that personal time." By prioritizing her life by what areas of her life she values most, Jenn is able to maintain the lifestyle she wants to live as a driven, working mom and avid life learner.

It takes one step outside of your comfort zone to change your life. What direction will you go?

Pearls of Wisdom:
- Organize your life with the same thought and care you would a well-balanced diet. Jean Thompson has learned, through many different seasons of her life, the importance of having patience with yourself and faith in your own abilities.
- Taking calculated risks has its pros and cons. In Nancy Outcalt's case, one risk landed her a husband yet another risk landed her at a company that didn't foster the healthy work-life balance she needed. Take

risks and understand you will get to your destination (maybe with a few missteps) at your own pace.

- It just takes one person to see your "light" and you are off to the races. Jenn found power in education and has used it to her advantage!

Chapter 3

Career First, Then Kids

"I don't like to be single-threaded in anything in my life."

—KIMBERLY DELLATORRE, BADASS TECHNOLOGY
SALESWOMAN, MOTHER OF THREE, WIFE,
VOLUNTEER, AND WORLD-TRAVELER.

ON LIVING A MULTI-THREADED LIFE

Living life in one dimension is nearly impossible. Life doesn't happen in a straight line. For Kimberly Della-Torre, it took twists and turns, ups and downs, and some lateral movement to get her to where she is today—a badass tech-saleswoman and hardworking mom of three.

Those two labels are only a fraction of Kimberly's story. The path traveled to arrive at those crowning accomplishments is long and riddled with big life-altering moments and choices.

CHOOSING A MOBILE LIFE

Kimberly graduated college in the middle of a recession. She worked whatever job she could to make ends meet and took full advantage of being young and fun in Hoboken. Yet, it wasn't enough. She looked around at her life, her boyfriend, her job, and wanted *more*. But what?

All her friends were getting engaged or married—starting new exciting chapters of their lives. She saw the trend and wanted to jump on board but in her own way. Instead of settling down, Kimberly packed up her world and moved out to California—leaving a relationship and her former life 3,000 miles in the dust.

After transferring to San Francisco and moving into a new role, Kimberly found success and personal growth in her new career and new life. She was constantly traveling for work and leisure, resulting in her passport being stamped on all continents by 2002—made possible by the airline miles she accrued through business trips and her sweet commission checks.

CHOOSING A COMMUNITY

"I was living on an airplane." Kimberly was consumed with work-travel and while that was exciting, it also exhausted her and left little room for a personal life. She desired a way to connect to her new city and find her new community and fast. Enter Junior League. "JLSF gave me some grounding and connection to the community. I wanted to go into fundraising, and I volunteered a lot. I did anything where I saw a need, including baby holding. When I moved out to California, the Junior League was another way of meeting more women."

The Junior League offered Kimberly the opportunity to explore her passion for volunteering, leadership, and giving back. This also expanded her tribe of like-minded women who shared her same devotion to bettering the community. "It gave me a whole new exposure to people I wouldn't have met or that would have taken me a lot longer to meet. My matron-of-honor was somebody I met very early on in the Junior League. We were on a committee together, and we just bonded."

Not only did Kimberly find lifelong friends, but she was also able to build her connection to a new city through the outreach and volunteer work done through the Junior League. Kimberly recalled, "I knew I wanted to focus on the community, and JLSF has always focused on that community level. Family preservation: homelessness, training, support, abuse... all of it! There were many opportunities to use current skills or develop new skills in a friendly training ground. For instance, fundraising: through large big events, I was able to put my selling skills to the test. I was basically selling goodwill."

Being able to apply her sales mindset to a good cause motivated Kimberly to continue her work with the Junior League. However, what really kept her involved on a personal level was the people and making a measurable difference. "I will say I met many great friends. I wouldn't trade the experience. It just gave me that sense of home when I was constantly on a plane."

CHOOSING A FAMILY

Work. Traveling. Volunteering. By all accounts, this move was a positive one for Kimberly. Yet, there was a nagging feeling that she was missing something...Kimberly knew she wanted to have kids. Many of her friends were either married long ago with kids or living up the single life in the Bay Area.

When she met her future husband, Kimberly's passport was maxed out. There was not a single page left to stamp. Ironically, she renewed her passport and ordered the one with a massive page count so she wouldn't encounter the same problem. Little did she know, she wouldn't get a single stamp for quite a while.

Three weeks before her fortieth birthday, Kimberly brought a beautiful little boy into the world. The second she had him, she knew she wanted another. Coming from a small family, it was important for her to build a bigger one for her children.

Kimberly is not alone in her decision to wait to have children until her late thirties.

As mentioned in *The Atlantic*, a study done by the Pew Research Center of the U.S Census Bureau data in 2016 revealed that more women are postponing the decision to have children until their late thirties and early forties, yet they are still choosing to ultimately have children. They choose this route due to their passionate pursuit of higher education and advancing their careers. As a result, the choice to have kids acts as a sort of "capstone to a life of education and labor.[4]" Kimberly did not stop at one child as most of the data suggests women having children at this age do. She wanted to give her son siblings.

---

4   Khazan, Olga. "The Rise Of Older Mothers". *The Atlantic*, 2018.

After several miscarriages and other challenges getting pregnant a second time, Kimberly sought out medical help. In-vitro proved to be the answer as she became pregnant with not just one baby but two!

With the growing number of their family, Kimberly and her husband decided out of "temporary insanity" to be near family. They packed up and moved clear across the country to Virginia to be in closer proximity to Kimberly's parents. Her eldest son was turning two years old and her twins were on the way!

It was no walk in the park bringing her twins into this world. Kimberly was on bed rest for two months straight because her pregnancy was at-risk. When she could, she tried to work from her bed—the beauty of high-level sales is that it can easily be done remotely. Work acted as an escape as she tried to distract herself from the confines of the hospital room.

The twins were on their own time schedule. They wanted to greet the world early. It was much too soon for any medically safe birth but they wouldn't wait. The doctors tried everything to persuade them otherwise. At twenty-seven weeks, the twins crashed into this world! They were considered micro-preemies and spent the first 100 days of their lives in the NICU.

Their recent move to Virginia was a product of divine intervention. "My twins were meant to be born here." Kimberly holds firm to that belief. They were born at one of the most recognized hospitals in the nation for neonatal care. It was a terrifying 100 days for both mom and babies. "I couldn't tell anyone. I couldn't even be excited because we weren't sure they would have a positive outcome—life. I stayed off social media. It was how I coped. Dad coped differently. He wanted to retain any hope he could." Today, the twins are happy and healthy, but that was the most emotionally turbulent, uncertain, and terrifying time in Kimberly's life. Her gratitude for that hospital's care is immense.

CHOOSING A LEGACY

In order to convey her gratitude for the help and care they received, Kimberly created an endowment fund for the Inova Fairfax Hospital NICU to help neonatal doctors and nurses support families in the NICU. Kimberly's act of giving back to the hospital that gave her twins a chance at life is the kind of positive reinforcement the world needs. Kimberly was well-equipped to identify a good cause and fill a need as a long-time philanthropic member of the Junior League and practiced saleswoman.

Speaking of her profession, her company's reaction to this heart-wrenching situation was admirable.

"There's no corporate plan that is written to support you in this scenario." Kimberly spoke very highly of her company at the time, saying, "The company was as great as it could possibly be." After being on bed rest in the hospital for two months, then dealing with the stress of having two babies in the NICU for 100 days, Kimberly was only able to stay home with her twins for two months. "They came home on Halloween, and I went back to work January 1st." Fortunately, her twins did not need any excessive care when they were out of the hospital, and at that point, Kimberly found the right combination of childcare help to make it possible for her to go back to work. "After having three kids, I needed to go back to work. It was expensive!"

Thankfully, Kimberly was not the sole provider of her household. Her husband works full-time for Hilton Global. "What sets us apart is that we are equals as breadwinners, equals in our professional lives, and equals in parenting." This balance is unique and carefully chosen.

When Kimberly and I were discussing her marriage, she had this to say on the topic of partnership: "I think for anyone—when they're selecting a life partner—it is important to consider who you want to go through the cycles of life with. What I mean by that is, if you get sick, or you have a parent who is sick, it's important to see how they react. How caring are they? If a friend has a baby, are they going to hold the baby? Are they willing to change it? Do they do their part of the laundry? What do they take care of and what do they put on you? Knowing how your life partner might be as a spouse and as a parent is really important. Typically, people don't change." At the core of her being, Kimberly believes it is important to know who your partner is, how they act, and what they bring to the table in a relationship before committing to them as the person you want to do life with.

It is important to find balance in your partnership. Kimberly was effusive in saying, "My husband is spectacular with our kids. We tag-team and prioritize the kids equally."

CHOOSING HER ADVENTURES

Kimberly remains authentic to herself and her desires in each new season of her life. She has committed to so many different aspects—volunteering, work, family—yet she attempts to maintain a healthy balance for herself.

Her version of self-care takes two forms—physical activity and social interaction. As an extremely social person who now lives in a more rural area, it takes more effort to see friends. She communicated her need for social interaction early on and all appreciate this element of her life. Even her kids know when "Mommy needs a playdate." A night out, a yoga retreat, or her annual girls' trips to Scottsdale and San Francisco.

To stay physically active in this season of her life, Kimberly has found an incredibly supportive community at her local yoga studio. Fun fact: stress is one of the most popular reasons people choose to practice yoga[5]. "It's a respite from the world. I sweat it out. I feel like me." United by their practice, Kimberly has found a lot of women to bond with through yoga. "It's been a real saving grace for me, the past fourteen or fifteen months. It is my happy place."

Yet this personal practice comes at the expense of something else and adds to that ever-present sense that, as a mom or as a professional, she could be doing more. Self-care to Kimberly took on a new meaning as a mom when she found herself just trying to squeeze in time for herself. "It comes with the feeling like I'm sacrificing time with

5   "Yoga Statistics: Staggering Growth Shows Ever-
     Increasing Popularity". *The Good Body*, 2018.

my kids or sacrificing doing something extra for work by not calling that one more customer. The prioritization and feeling like am I being too selfish? These are my own personal struggles that get interjected all too often."

Kimberly has found that, at any given age, there is a give-and-take to life. Yet she has never been "single-threaded" as she described her lifestyle to me. Kimberly has made it a point to participate in multiple areas of her life at once in order to feel fulfilled. In her case, making the move for a job to California to fill her work "glass" was a huge leap of faith in her career. That move brought instability in her personal life, as she was in a new place where she needed to find a new community. In joining the Junior League, she was able to craft a new community for herself and contribute to her philanthropic goals at the same time. As a mom, Kimberly is constantly repaving the path to continue to crush it at work while feeling like she is spending enough time with her kids, and that road has many twists and turns. Kimberly's younger son was recently diagnosed with the learning disability dyslexia. Dyslexia affects one in five people. It has been a new learning opportunity for Kimberly as a mom, and she dove headfirst into the challenge of educating herself on the subject.

Defining her own boundaries in these separate areas has helped her to be able to divide her time while still dedicating time to the areas she deems most important. Kimberly has built her own multi-threaded lifestyle over time. Rome was not built in a day, and in the same way, it is impossible to experience all that life has to offer at the same time.

Be the architect of your own life—weave your threads accordingly. Don't be afraid to untie a knot when necessary!

Pearls of Wisdom:
- Changing cities means the opportunity to grow a new community! Be intentional. Find a group that shares your values. Be active in your pursuit.
- Test drive your partner before you buy. How do they react in situations that involve children, work stress, and illness? Do they do laundry? All are important data points to gather before you go full Beyoncé and put a ring on it!
- Self-care is essential to mental health when you are running 100 miles per hour. Find out what helps you decompress and determine how you need to recharge to be able to show up for the people in your life at full power. It might look like yoga or happy hour with a close friend—whatever is authentic to what you need!

Chapter 4

No Kids Required

"I don't think I've missed out on anything in my life. I've been able to put my energy and resources toward the people and causes that really matter to me and that has been the ultimate reward."

—MELINDA THOMAS, COO OF OCTAVE BIOSCIENCE

There are so many paths in life and not all lead to parenthood. In 2018, *Morning Consult for The New York Times* conducted a poll[6] of close to 2,000 people ranging in age from twenty to forty-five. Thirty-six percent of survey respondents said they did not have kids and were not interested in having kids for various reasons. Some wanted more leisure time. Others hadn't found

---

6   Pitofsky, Marina. "'It's Just Not For Me': Why A Growing Number Of Women Are Saying No To Parenthood". *Usatoday.Com*, 2019.

the right partner to start a family with at that point in their lives. The financial responsibility of raising children was another powerful factor under close consideration.

I want to showcase four women who are living extremely fulfilling lives sans kids. Each of them has committed to her passions, strives toward mastery of her own individual *art*, and has built a family in her own way.

THE ART OF SHOWING UP

Meet Melinda Thomas.

She is a badass biotech leader and founder, and a dedicated volunteer. At forty-six years old, she added loving wife, thoughtful dog mom, and stepmother of two teenage girls into the mix. On top of all of those responsibilities, Melinda is able to prioritize and support her three siblings, parents, and nine nieces and nephews.

Melinda's busy personal and professional lives demand that she constantly wear different hats. Through it all, she stays focused on her two core drivers:

- Getting Stuff Done: With so much on her plate, Melinda has come up with a system to focus her efforts and bring her goals to fruition.

- Showing Up Where There is Need: Melinda is motivated to show up for those people and causes that need her particular skill set.

By zeroing in on these two goals, Melinda has accomplished some seriously powerful things from an authentic place. The secret sauce to her success is the "One to Many Principle." It works by taking an active break by doing one mind-numbingly boring activity that serves to help check many boxes. Her reasoning behind this method is that, "it is very important to clear your mind in order to give it a chance to work on a problem."

Several days a week, Melinda will leave the office around 3 PM to either go for a swim, ride her bike, or hike The Dish near Stanford Campus. Before she leaves work, she will often pre-load a problem into her brain to think about while she exercises. Whether it is a business problem or an upcoming milestone for a family member, Melinda gets her best thinking accomplished on the move. "With all the blood pumping, I get a lot of mental work done. I see and solve problems. That whole thing for your mom for Mother's Day was done on a bike ride."

TEAMWORK MAKES THE DREAM WORK

Full disclosure, I happen to be one of the nine lucky nieces and nephews Melinda rains all of her love and affection on. She called me one day out of the blue and said, "Drew, I have an idea for your mom." It was a month before the Mother's Day that marked my mother's twentieth year as a wonderful momma. It was also the last Mother's Day she would have a kid at home, as my younger sister left for college the next year. She was in the end-stages of completing a milestone in her parenting career. My aunt had the idea to formally recognize my mom in a business-awards-style ceremony.

Before kids, my mom was an MBA-toting badass businesswoman. She consistently won awards such as a trip to Jamaica and earned an engraved champagne bucket for her efforts. My mom was used to being recognized for her hard work in the business world. When she pivoted to staying at home—because my sister and I were a full-time job...let me tell you—that formal recognition process evaporated. Yes, on Mother's Day, we wrote her wonderful cards and gave her memorable gifts. It wasn't the same as getting up in front of the top performers in your company and having them all applaud you. Plus, the awards rocked! Who doesn't want to go to Jamaica? My aunt recognized this hole in the stay-at-home mom role and found an incredibly special way to recognize and applaud my mom's success as a mother by giving her back the public kudos she deserved.

All of us wrote speeches, my aunt hosted the award presentation, a crystal engraved wine stopper was presented to her, and the cutest slideshow played. In our speeches, we presented her with all the roles she held from Auction Chair to Team Mom and gave her shining performance reviews. Needless to say, there were many happy tears shed. None of that would have happened if it weren't for one bike ride and Melinda's talented abilities to pull people together to achieve a common goal and identify a need and fill it.

BEING THE HEAD CHEERLEADER

Throughout her career, Melinda has been in charge of molding and shaping company cultures. As the COO and Co-Founder of Octave Bioscience, Melinda set the tone and built out a collaborative, all-in culture from the start. Recently, the team has been killing it—aligning on common goals, hitting targets, earning new certifications, and hiring like crazy!

A concern with such fast-paced growth is how to maintain the integrity of a well-established company culture. Melinda spun on this problem while she swam laps. The team had just earned an important certification that opened up whole new opportunities for lab testing, and she wanted to reward their efforts. It was important to Melinda that her employees feel their contribution seen and valued by the company.

On a Sunday night, Melinda snuck into the office with a bunch of balloons. Each person who slaved away on the important certification walked in Monday morning to find a fun balloon pinned to their chair. Later that afternoon, her colleague approached her and thanked her for the gesture.

Melinda was surprised. "How did you know it was me?"

The woman replied, "Of course, it was you! You are the head cheerleader."

She does all of this out of her genuine desire to celebrate others successes. The balloons functioned to make those individuals feel good about their contribution in addition to reinforcing the core values of the company. Creating and communicating this positive feedback loop sets the tone for hard work and effort, as well as challenges those in management positions to adopt her techniques to continue to inspire their direct reports.

Melinda shows up in big ways for those in her life, whether it be her family or her colleagues. She works hard at cultivating these relationships and aspires to make others feel seen and appreciated. Operating through the "One to Many Principle," Melinda has found a way to accomplish her goals while supporting those around her and taking care of herself.

THE ART OF VALUES-BASED PRIORITIZATION

Meet Jill Boltmann.

This woman is an awesome career media professional who strives to inspire the next generation of salespeople. Her passion for mentoring young professionals is born out of the help she received from her own mentors.

Jill commented on her path to finding her dream job, "I thought I wanted to work in public relations. I told that to the HR director of a major television network affiliate in Seattle, and she promptly told me she was 'putting me in sales.' I was shocked, but it put me on a course with my dream job, which I landed at twenty-seven and stayed in for twenty years. Sometimes, the best career advice comes from the unlikeliest of sources—in my case, a virtual stranger. There was a less-than-dreamy job before the dream job but that gave me several mentors who were absolutely instrumental in helping me land the dream job and with whom I'm very close with to this day." Finding a community that supports and pushes you to show up as your best self is integral to personal success. This is no easy task. It takes effort, lots of coffee meet-ups, and providing value in return to those who extend their hand to help you as you create this kind of supportive *built network*.

THE BUILT NETWORK

A *built network* is one that is carefully curated for a purpose and is easily accessible. In this case, Jill was interested in learning more about the media industry and needed to get the inside scoop from those in similar roles. It requires a strong foundation built on deep relationships. Surface-level networking won't get you where you need to go when it comes to cultivating a built network. A surface-level connection does not understand your goals, your personal and professional history, and how in combination they have shaped you and informed your decision-making. The purpose of a built network is to create an arsenal of people who are willing to do battle for you to help get you where you want to be!

To this day, Jill is still in touch with those who helped guide her at that early stage in her career. She is always quick to give them props for the role they played in helping her discover what she really wanted to do when she "grew up." She makes it a top priority to reach out and stay in touch with them. In fact, many years later, she had the good fortune of working at the same company and in the same department with one of those mentors.

THE RETURN ON A BUILT NETWORK

Media sales ages people in "dog years," and the pressure to perform is incredible. This high-stress job is paid one hundred percent on commission, meaning your livelihood is never guaranteed. "There were many sleepless nights that just weren't healthy. I took an informal vow of silence every day when I came home from work because I was so drained." Jill ended up having to leave a volunteer role at Make-A-Wish that she loved so that she could keep her head above water.

After twenty years, Jill was emotionally and physically exhausted. That burnout, combined with the death of her mother, made her reexamine everything in her life. In an effort to regain sanity, she decided to take an eight-month sabbatical so she could get back to a place where she felt recharged both physically and emotionally.

After several work-free months, Jill wanted a project to occupy her mind. Serendipitously, a friend of hers worked as the publicist for a rock band and tapped Jill to help with a few upcoming projects. Getting back to work allowed her to see some people she really missed and exercise the marketing side of her brain, giving her a sense of purpose. You can never predict the opportunities that will fall into your lap when you have a well-built network. At this point in her life, she prioritized her health and getting back to her center. By taking a sabbatical, Jill gave herself the gift of a safe space to reconnect her values and goals and realign them with her professional life. Getting to work with a killer band was a fringe benefit!

PURSUING PROJECTS ALIGNED WITH VALUES

When she returned to the workforce, Jill found a company and a role that satisfied her desire to learn something new and different in the media industry she loved. The company also afforded her a better work-life balance. When her father was ill, Jill was able to spend more quality time with him and help with daily care. In this season of her life, and on the heels of losing her mom, prioritizing time with family ranked over work, and she found the opportunity to balance the two.

In 2015, she was approached by a client of hers with an offer she couldn't refuse. He asked Jill to join his media and marketing company in a business development role. She saw an opportunity to stretch her thinking, learn from a savvy professional, and work with someone she respected and held in very high regard. Jill is naturally curious and sees learning new things as a way of life. Experiencing life as a marketing consultant in this new season of her career was a challenge, full of teachable moments, and she's discovered so much about herself in the process.

If you take anything away from Jill's story, I hope you see how important it is to make time for yourself and for those you love and respect. As you prioritize yourself and your valued relationships, you will gain insight into where you to invest your energy going forward. Trusting in those mentors and advisors will take you places and provide you opportunities you never before imagined. Create a *built network* authentically!

THE ART OF BUILDING NEW PLATFORMS
Meet Jen Wisbey.

Jen is actually a part of Jill Boltmann's built network. Small world! The two met at the same high-stress, high-stakes media sales company. Before Jen found Jill, she struggled to find women within the company who truly wanted to see other women succeed. Jen illustrated the experience as, "There was a lot of throwing elbows and not much leaning on shoulders." Due to the competitive environment, she even threw a few elbows herself in an effort to prove herself. It was the nature of the beast.

TURNING NEGATIVE INTO POSITIVE

She chose to rise above. "It was not an easy row to hoe." It was a constant battle between maintaining her integrity and taking the easy way out. Jen found herself at a crossroads. She witnessed a situation that wasn't right and had to put her hand up and call out the toxic behavior. Her integrity would not let her ignore it. After going through all the proper reporting processes, no action was taken to correct the culture problem at that organization. Instead of removing herself from the situation, Jen stayed. As a manager, she promised a few colleagues on her team that she would not abandon them. In hindsight, she wishes she would have bowed out.

Ultimately, four years later, Jen was fired. She felt strongly about standing up and sharing her concerns about the direction of the company. This bold action caused her to fall out of favor with decision-makers. It was difficult for her to conceptualize the idea of leaving the company. She'd spent twenty-one years there and was one of few women in a high-level managerial role. Jen recalled, "At the time, it was hard to think of walking away. Being fired felt like being hit over the head with a shovel. Now that I am out though, my life is one hundred percent better." She highlighted that in this new season of her life, she has regained her self-worth and rebuilt her self-esteem. Jen is on to new adventures. "I fit the job I worked for twenty-five years just fine, but I belong in the life I'm living since I left!"

Jen saw a problem with the company culture, and she also saw a path that might lead to a solution. However, the company's decision to actively ignore the culture problem motivated Jen to do more research and determine what elements made up a positive company culture. She was fascinated by the employee contribution on an individual level to the greater collective. Through her experiences and her research, she found that, like most things in life, the level of effort an employee exerts toward company culture correlates directly to success and happiness of the employee and the greater good of the organization. The more effort they put in, the more they get out! Other elements she researched and refined had to do with understanding the difference between managers and leaders within a company and the roles they play as well as outlining career paths for employees. All of these elements of culture and how they blended together to make or break an organization fascinated Jen.

"You must be the change you wish to see in the world."
—Gandhi[7]

Gandhi's famous quote kept echoing in her mind as she continued to educate herself on the topic. That one negative experience sparked a new passion and a new business endeavor. Jen got together with a friend and crafted an entire consulting brand focused on assessing and redesigning company culture. That isn't her only brainchild. Once Jen got a sweet taste of entrepreneurship, she sought out more opportunities to build new platforms.

JEN THE BUILDER

Her background in media, music, and entertainment led her to two other exciting ventures that play into her passions.

The first is the West Seattle Beer and Music Festival. It takes an incredible amount of logistical planning and

---

7   "A Quote By Mahatma Gandhi". *Goodreads.Com*, 2019.

coordination to put on a music festival, let alone make it profitable. She partnered with a beer connoisseur to curate limited barrels of popular local craft breweries to draw the community and provide a special place for beer and music lovers. "Seattle is the mecca of places to do this, with the sheer quantity of craft breweries we have in the area." Any opportunity to taste something you can't find in the grocery store is special. Calling on local companies to sponsor the event has been a great exercise of her sales experience earlier in her career.

The second business venture Jen is getting up and running is a party planning company. Her passion for the West Seattle Beer and Music Festival helped her realize the fulfillment she got from creating a space where people can enjoy themselves. "We know a good party when we see one, so we've decided to go out and make that happen for those who don't have the ability to fully actualize their party planning vision." This serves as another way Jen is exercising her professional talents alongside her passions.

In pursuing her passions, Jen surrounded herself with purpose-driven people. She's seen the difference they can make. "Purposeful people can't be stopped. They are mission-driven and everything they do is for the greater good." By surrounding herself with these people, their push for purpose rubbed off on her, and she was inspired to build her own projects out in the world.

She is a true believer that if you love what you do, there is no such thing as work-life balance. According to Jen, "There doesn't need to be lines drawn if what you love fulfills you both personally and professionally." Find what's important to you in life and pour yourself into it whole-heartedly.

THE ART OF FILLING UP YOUR CUP

Meet Carolyn Kelly.

She is the perfect example of why you should take a practice interview seriously. Fresh out of graduate school, Carolyn interviewed at *The Seattle Times* in the accounting department. She didn't even really want the job going into the interview but figured it would be good practice in her job search. She was offered the role and a short thirty-three years later, she retired from the CEO role.

Carolyn finds fulfillment in new challenges, uses failures as learning moments to navigate murky waters, and *always* stays true to her values. Her sustaining life force is her 5:30 AM running habit, and she believes the secret to a happy life is healthy living. She is living proof that you don't have to have children to leave a legacy.

A SERVANT LEADER HEART

In her years at *The Seattle Times*, Carolyn's favorite part of the job was making an impact locally. "I just loved being involved in the community across all different strata." The motto of the paper at the time was "serving the community through quality journalism," and Carolyn's mission was to deliver on that promise.

When asked about why she was so passionate about helping, informing, and uplifting communities, she traced the origin all the way back to her childhood. She grew up in a very Catholic family. Her parents were very actively engaged in the church they went to and also in the neighborhood she grew up in. They reinforced the value of contributing to something beyond yourself in her formative years, and Carolyn believes that primary exposure to community building nurtured this fledgling passion in her. It was again reinforced in her Jesuit education. Ideals of servant leadership were taught, and she soaked up all the information she could learn.

At *The Seattle Times*, she worked across so many different departments. She understood so many facets of the business knew she could help guide the company. She was so active on non-profit boards and community organizations at this time and still is to this day. Any way she can make an impact, she pours her time and energy into uplifting the Greater Seattle community.

TEST OF CHARACTER

"The Seattle Times had some really dark days." Carolyn spoke of a challenge that arose several years back. The foundational integrity of the business and her own personal values were jeopardized. She stuck to her guns and fell back on her mission to serve the community. "I would rather have failed doing that than lied and tried to skirt the truth." By holding true to the mission of the company and her own personal values, Carolyn was able to help guide *The Seattle Times* away from potential bankruptcy and back on track.

Shortly after she was able to help steady the waters at *The Seattle Times,* Carolyn made the decision to retire. She was confident she was leaving it in good hands and on the right path. She considered staying a few more years but after weighing the options, she opted to get out of the way and let future leaders take over. Upon her retirement, the larger Seattle business community was certain she would find a new COO position elsewhere. However, six weeks into her new retirement, Carolyn knew she would never go back to a full-time job ever again.

Today Carolyn sits on a number of boards for charitable and for-profit organizations helping the community in ways she is extremely passionate about, championing change. In these roles, she has the privilege to work with incredible, intelligent, kind-hearted people who share the same passion for community and social change. Carolyn is a great example of surrounding yourself with interesting people who will enrich your life and fill your cup so you can continue to serve others.

Pearls of Wisdom:
- Through Melinda Thomas, we learned fulfillment can come from all different areas of your life and you can make a profound impact.
  One to Many Principle
- Jill Boltmann showcased that taking time off for yourself and for those you love is a great way to hit the refresh button on your perspective on life.
  Built networks have high return on investment.
- Find what's important to you in life and pour (pun intended) yourself into it whole-heartedly just like Jen Wisbey.
  If you love what you do then you'll never work a day in your life.

- Take from Carolyn Kelly's experience and surround yourself with interesting people who will enrich your life and fill your cup so you can continue to serve others.

Curate your close circle. They help you grow!

Chapter 5

Leveraging a Community

"No one puts Baby in a corner."

—PATRICK SWAYZE AS JOHNNY CASTLE

IN THE MOVIE *Dirty Dancing*[8]

While this scene is equal parts hot and heartwarming, the simple truth is that in life, people will try to define you at every turn. Often in the way of labels. Think about it. You can label a person six ways to Sunday if you really go for it. Race, religion, body type, eye color, whatever

---

8   a Lionsgate presentation ; in association with Great American Films Limited Partnership ; produced by Linda Gottlieb ; written by Eleanor Bergstein ; directed by Emile Ardolino. *Dirty Dancing*. Santa Monica, Calif. :Lionsgate, 2010.

your personality type is according to Myers-Briggs, and more. One of the longest standing "corners" we often get boxed into is being female. Shannon Vetto was raised in an environment that reinforced that women did not have as much potential as men.

VETO FROM VETTO

Spoiler Alert: Patrick Swayze does not come to the rescue. The girl saves herself in this one... with some help from a few people along the way.

WORDS MATTER

"I grew up with a father that didn't know any better," says Vetto as she reflects on how her upbringing fueled her drive. "One of the things he always said to me was, 'You don't invest in the girls.' Despite the fact that he was willing to put me through college, as he was very much into education and academics, he was raised in a generation where women never worked. So he gave me the education, but he didn't necessarily think I'd ever do anything with it." As a graduate of the University of Washington with a degree in Accounting, Shannon armed herself with the knowledge she needed to succeed. "I just remember a lot of that language as a kid and I remember thinking,

'I can show him.'" She laughed as if it were ridiculous that anyone could think otherwise. "I can do anything!"

With that attitude, Shannon, equipped with a checks and balances based education, moved to Boston with the goal of becoming a (wait for it)... fashion designer. "I wanted to be the next Calvin Klein or Vera Wang."

When she was offered a job in Boston at Pricewaterhouse-Coopers (PwC) post-graduation, Shannon jumped at the opportunity. Boston was close enough to New York and not as scary. The plan was to work for a few years at PwC until she landed her first fashion job. To her surprise, Shannon fell in love with her job as a public accountant. "I was a CPA, and it was viewed as that flagship role by my parents. My dad, in particular, was super proud." He would walk around with her business cards and tell everyone his daughter was a CPA for PwC. Her father adopted that mantra and repeated it to anyone who would listen to him.

Early in her life, Shannon struggled with feelings of resentment toward her father. "At the time, I thought he didn't believe in me but that really wasn't the case." By having limited exposure to working women and their success, Shannon's father did not have a baseline of understanding against which he could measure his daughter's goals. "It was more of a cultural thing. I see that now he has probably been my biggest supporter along the way." Yet, it was her father's commentary that lit her spark and solidified her drive.

TRAVEL TAKES YOU PLACES

Public accounting is a difficult job. Shannon traveled constantly and every few weeks she found herself in a new city examining a new business problem. The level of problem-solving and critical thinking necessary to consult on a company's financials hooked Shannon. She did not let a narrow-minded focus on a future in fashion prevent her from being present in her role. Shannon decided to have fun exploring her newfound passion as a Certified Public Accountant.

Even though she loved it, traveling ten months a year really throws a wrench in your personal life. When she met the man she knew she would marry in Seattle, Shannon decided it was time to look for her next job. "It felt like I was giving up because public accounting was seen as the hard job," said Vetto of her transition to working for one of her clients, Russell Investments. "I thought I was waving the white flag by moving into a private job. Russell Investments in Tacoma wasn't a flashy name in the investments industry at the time, but it was the only one in Seattle. It was slim pickings from that standpoint." Long story short, Shannon ended up working for Russell Investments for twenty years, helping them grow their business both domestically and internationally.

Making that level of impact on a company did not happen overnight. Shannon fought tooth and nail in a male-dominated industry to be able to make her wave. The way to make a name for yourself within the company was through international assignments. An opportunity to open a division in Japan came across her desk. It was identical to one Shannon had previously completed in Australia with flying colors. She knew she was capable of making this assignment a success.

With each international assignment, Shannon was able to diversify her experience and build a wealth of newfound strategic knowledge. Shannon jumped at the opportunity. She knew she had the know-how, and it could only help to reinforce her strengths in the eyes of her male peers.

Japan was a two-year assignment. Build. Launch. Grow. That was the game plan. It would mean flying back and forth from Seattle and weeks at a time away from her husband. It was going to be a big deal for whoever landed it. "It meant you were being groomed for greater things." She had to practically beg for it—she wanted it that badly. Shannon was pregnant at the time the project was announced, and she didn't advertise it. "I didn't want to tell anyone because I was afraid that it would be a reason not to give it to me." She worked hard on her plan to make the Japan launch a homerun. Her commitment to the project and dedication to replicating her success was palpable.

When it came down to making the decision on who would take point for the Japan project, Shannon went to the executive in charge. She felt obligated to tell him her secret. Confidently, she explained, "I know I can do this assignment. I want it so badly, but in full disclosure, before you make this decision, I need you to know I'm pregnant and the due date of my baby is April 15th."

His response to her was, "Perfect, the part of the assignment requiring you to be physically in Japan will be over by then. We're launching this project April 1st. I want you in this thing. You show all signs of getting it, and you're dedicated."

Shannon responded resolutely, "I promise you, I will finish this assignment."

When she got to Japan and dove headfirst into the project, it became apparent that the April 1st deadline to launch was not as firm as she hoped. "As we got closer to the delivery deadline, there was talk of pushing it out to June 30th. I said, 'Hang on! There is one deadline I can't push!'"

Shannon worked all the way up until her 35th week of pregnancy. In her 36th week, she was on the plane back to Seattle with a doctor's note in hand. While in flight, she experienced contractions and was truly afraid she would give birth mid-air somewhere over the Pacific Ocean. Finally, she landed at SeaTac, and Shannon went straight to the hospital only to find out they were Braxton Hicks. Maybe stress-induced?

Her due date came, and a beautiful baby girl joined the world. Unfortunately for Shannon, that meant the launch date for the Japan project was right around the corner. Even though she was overjoyed about her daughter's arrival, Shannon was disappointed to not be in Japan for the launch. "I really wanted to be there! On launch day, we moved $1 billion from a large bank into our new business division. That large of a transfer of money has a lot of accounting and detail issues that you can't anticipate. You have to problem-solve on the fly! It's the best part."

Shannon expressed that very sentiment to the executive who'd given her the job. His response shocked her... "Can you come?"

Ideas shot through her mind, trying to think of ways to make the trip to Japan work. "Not without the baby, I can't. I'm still nursing."

Immediately, all hands hit the deck. A colleague in the Seattle office, who also had a young child, lent Shannon his nanny. Three business-class seats were booked. A passport was issued for the six-week baby in under twenty-four hours. The next day, Shannon got on the plane and made it to Japan just in time for launch day.

She remembers the chaos of launch day vividly. "I was running back to the hotel room to pump then to the launch and then back to the hotel room." Shannon recounted the overwhelming feeling of support from all the men in the room. "They had children of their own; they were just so grateful that I was willing to be there."

The Japan project was one of the most successful businesses Russell Investments ever launched, and it was all orchestrated by a "crazy" pregnant lady. Her success and the wild story surrounding it got visibility all the way up to the CEO level. Let that sink in.

Upon reflection, Shannon doesn't really suggest this as the best practice for new mothers. However, it was what she needed in that moment. She is forever grateful the Russell team was willing to let her be a woman and a mother and help her see the project through until the end. The unwavering support she received was a testament to the trust they had in her ability to pull a feat like this off. They made this happen at a time when she was still at the manager level of the business. Only later would she join the ranks of director and keep climbing!

EMPLOYING A PERSONAL BOARD OF DIRECTORS

Shannon spent nineteen wonderful years with the Russell Investments Team. When they were acquired by the London Stock Exchange, she suddenly found herself looking for her next adventure. Without a job and without any idea where to look next, Shannon went through an identity crisis. Her job had been such a powerful piece of her identity that she had to do some soul searching to understand what this next phase meant, not only in advancing her career but also for her personal development.

"The hardest transition I ever made was the one where I left my highly-coveted, very powerful job at a firm that I loved. I had no idea what I was going to do next, but I knew it was going to be different. It was emotionally very hard to be laid off—I kept calling it my radical sabbatical to avoid coming to terms with the truth—and recovering from that required a lot of work with my Personal Board of Directors."

At a fork in the road, unable to determine which path to take, Shannon turned to her trusted advisors—her *Personal Board of Directors* as she calls them—and sought their wise counsel and knowledgeable advice. They know her well and were able to be frank, honest, and no BS regarding what came next in her professional life. One such board member advised her to take a year, network her heart out, and see what opportunities arose that piqued her interest. "I keep people who remind me how to tackle my fears on my Personal Board of Directors. They give me the hard advice at professional junctures in my life that I know I can trust."

By turning to these trusted people in her life, Shannon was able to take the first shaky step in a new direction off her beaten path and ultimately find success. Of course, that came after one or two major roadblocks that left her questioning her life decision. When doubt crept in,

Shannon's Personal Board of Directors were there to pick her up, dust her off, and orient her course.

NEW QUEEN IN TOWN

Shannon fell into the investment side of the cannabis industry. She adamantly states, "I really truly believe it is going to be as big as the .com boom!"

Looking back at her professional crossroads, if someone had told Shannon that in just two years, she would be viewed as a pretty neat person in the cannabis industry, she would never have envisioned that for herself. "I would have told them they were smoking dope!"

Now branded the Cannabis Queen and the Marijuana Whisperer, Shannon is a thought leader within the cannabis industry. She consults for top brands as well as mentors young entrepreneurs in the space to help them build the confidence to be successful. She appeared on a panel at an event where Howard Schultz was the keynote speaker. She discussed the current investment trends in the cannabis industry, the how and why behind investing, and more. "In the audience were some of the most powerful women from across the nation, and I was sitting there going 'holy shit!' I hate public speaking."

Her incredible journey as a cannabis strategist, mentor, and speaker would never have been possible without the advice and support from her Personal Board of Directors. Cultivate yours intentionally.

Pearls of Wisdom:
- Don't let other people's limited thinking change the scope of your dreams. Use them as inspiration to reach higher!
- Find people you trust to be your cheerleaders, your mentors, the reality check you need when you need it most. These people can help guide you in order to prevent you from learning mistakes the hard way. Their gift to you is being able to bounce ideas around before taking action and knowing to take their advice. Of course, they are right... you picked them!

Part Two

There is Strength In Community

Chapter 6

Growing Your Community

"We are always better when we're together!"

—*Better Together* BY JACK JOHNSON[9]

FINDING YOUR PEOPLE (AT ANY STAGE OF LIFE)

Meet Christine Baerwaldt. Bad-ass saleswoman, mother, wife, and committed friend.

One of the hardest things to do in life is to live up to your own expectations. Christine has set the bar high

9   Lyrics.com, STANDS4 LLC, 2019. "Better Together Lyrics." Accessed June 2, 2019.

on the type of friend, partner, and mother she strives to be. Her approach is values-backed and intentional. Most importantly, Christine's methodical approach forming and maintaining relationships is genuine.

KEEPING YOUR GALS CLOSE

Graduating from college, Christine had an amazing group of friends that she chose to spend her time with. By choosing to invest her time with these ladies, there was some serious effort involved on all sides to keep the crew together. Christine recalls, "In the first four years after we graduated, we had weekly *Grey's Anatomy* potlucks... back when it first got big. Over time, that dwindled because some of the group's values shifted. They focused on their career or chose to invest their time elsewhere, but we still get together once a month and make that time for each other." Her group of college friends doesn't look the same today as it did when she first graduated yet the intentional cadence with which she sees those college friends remains to this day.

"For lack of better words, I don't want to be my mother's generation where I only have two or three friends. I still want to be getting together with my group of thirty friends when I'm seventy years old," Christine shared candidly. She doesn't want to play just a numbers game.

Christine gravitates toward those women who share similar values to her own and who are balancing a career as well as a family. When you only have so much time, it is important to spend it with those friends who truly celebrate your wins with you and empathize with your struggles. By intentionally choosing the friends she spends her time with, and ensuring their values align, Christine is able to curate the energy around her in a powerful way. When her circle of friends is likeminded, they build each other up and help each other out as they flow through similar seasons in life. Of her college crew, Christine highlighted, "Continuing the longevity of those friendships is one of my main focuses because they are so meaningful to me."

BRINGING NEW FRIENDS INTO THE FOLD

When you move to a new place, it is hard to start over even if it is just a new part of town. Christine was adamant about building a community not only for herself but for her family in their new neighborhood. "I made a very valid point, which was a bit awkward at times, to introduce myself to anybody I saw who had a child of similar age to my own." It worked! She was able to spark friendships with an incredible network of moms all within a mile radius of her house. "There are five families within a mile proximity of our house that we get together with on a regular basis, whether it be with the kids or just us moms going out for a drink!"

This bold approach to creating her incredible new network of moms in her area was born out of the skills she learned networking in business. "I took those same networking skills that I'd learned in business and interjected them into my personal life to try to drive those new relationships." Christine was very intentional in how she went about forming these new relationships in her community and continues to be thoughtful in carving out time to spend with her neighborhood community. Because Christine places such a high value on cultivating her community, it takes up a great deal of her time outside of work. Luckily, she has help in making it happen.

KNOWING WHAT YOU SIGNED UP FOR

"My husband knew what he was signing up for." Christine laughs. The two met in college at the University of Washington. "He saw how I was with my friends and knew how important that aspect of my life was to me way before we got married." She credits a great deal of her ability to invest in other relationships outside of her family to her husband.

"I have a very supportive other half who has allowed me to invest so much time in my career and in relationships outside of just our family." To name a few ways her husband supports her to make this happen, Christine mentioned that her husband will pick up the kids frequently and happily manage them while she has a girl's night with friends, even if it's the night before she leaves on a work trip. She and her husband are very clear on their own individual needs when it comes to how they invest their time and work to set clear expectations with each other. This open line of communication has been a lifeline in building a life for herself that incorporates those things most important to her—her family, career, and maintaining friendships.

Just as she is intentional in building and maintaining friendships, Christine was intentional about how she designed her life with her partner. She recognizes that she can't divide herself into equal parts across the important facets of her life. "Everything takes sacrifice. It's just a matter of maneuvering all the different facets of your life to actually work together and being real with your time."

WHAT MAKES A TRUE PARTNERSHIP?

Meet Suzanne Salzberg. Mother, wife of thirty-four years, amateur chef, and passionate career advisor.

THINK LONG-TERM

There have been many seasons to Suzanne's career. She found a career in recruiting straight out of college that played perfectly into her focus in school and has stuck with it ever since. Her favorite part is helping candidates prep for the interview. Before she chose to pursue recruiting, Suzanne was offered a role in sales at Procter & Gamble. Reflecting back on the offer, she admits she probably would have taken the job had her now husband of thirty-four years not started there a year earlier. "We would have had to move to LA to make sure we didn't overlap territories. When I really got to thinking about it, I was always going to be a year behind him. At Procter & Gamble, on the fast track, you get promoted every year or two and usually relocated with the promotion. When he was getting promoted, I would be just starting a new role. It would have been off-balance for our relationship."

She decided that it was not the way she wanted to start her married life and instead took a job she could do from anywhere. "I can be in a boat in the middle of the water and recruit as long as I have my phone. It's perfect for our lifestyle." When her husband got promoted to the headquarters' office of Procter and Gamble, Suzanne, along with a one-year-old daughter, had to pack up their life and move to Cincinnati. In this season of her life, she decided to put a pause on her career and focus on grounding her family in this new city.

SEEK VALUE

Suzanne got really active in her new community, taking on volunteer roles that quickly snowballed into leadership roles with lots of responsibility. "Even when I was at home, I would seek out roles like PTA President. I would approach these roles like a business career. We would talk about it in that way. My husband valued my job and we would bounce ideas off each other because we both enjoyed talking about our careers with each other." She commented that it wasn't ever a negative for either of them to bring up work as a topic of discussion. They thoroughly enjoyed sharing how they spent their time and sought advice from the other to help solve problems. "We both valued what each other did equally and that enabled us to have great conversations."

Her husband valued Suzanne's choice to stay at home because he saw the value it added to their daughters' lives and their family dynamic as a whole. Suzanne candidly said, "He would tell me, 'You have the harder job and I value what you are doing for our family so much.' It is that kind of recognition and appreciation that creates an equal partnership." Her husband put Suzanne's happiness in front of his own for the next season of their life together, and he was genuine about doing so. Suzanne felt secure in knowing that whatever she ventured to pursue her husband would back her one hundred percent because he knew what she was capable of regardless of the title of her role.

PRIORITIZE YOUR PARTNER'S HAPPINESS

After her daughters went off to college, Suzanne and her husband had a choice to make. Her husband was offered another promotion in another city, but when he presented the opportunity to Suzanne, he prefaced it by saying it was her turn. Years earlier, she packed up her life to support her husband's career, and now he was willing to do the same for her. As a team, they decided to move back to Seattle, and Suzanne continued her interview consulting career, running her customized apparel business and reignited her recruiting consulting career, working for many *Fortune 500* companies as well as several hot startups.

She and her husband continue to talk shop over the dinner table and play on many of the same sports teams. Overall, Suzanne admits, "We truly enjoy each other's company." The secret sauce to a true partner comes down to finding that person who wants your happiness more than their own and sees value in everything you do. Suzanne is adamant that those three elements—enjoying spending time with one another, putting your partner's happiness before your own, and seeing value in all that your partner does... "It's huge. That doesn't mean maintaining that partnership isn't hard work but having that foundation makes you want to work for it!"

According to Suzanne, it is possible to Have It All, just not necessarily all at the same time. Different aspects of life will ebb and flow in different seasons of your life. Her husband says, "It is all about the mix." Life is about finding that perfect mix. An equal partnership starts with a great foundation. Communicate with your partner and decide together how you will live your joint life as a team!

TERMS AND CONDITIONS MAY APPLY

Meet JoAnne Kennedy. VP of Technology at Nordstrom (and business leader at many other *Fortune 500* companies before that), mother of four, and wife to a wonderful stay-at-home dad.

ESTABLISHING A WORKABLE CONTRACT

When JoAnne and her husband first started building their family, both of them worked corporate full-time jobs that were very important to them. At the beginning, when her first two children were two and three years old, when both parents were at work, JoAnne's mom could pinch-hit when they needed her. When the kids got sick, their ad hoc plan started to fail them. "You can't send sick kids off to daycare, and my mom couldn't stay home with them all day. It just wasn't working anymore."

She and her husband sat down with the goal of playing calendar chess to try to come up with an effective game plan going forward. JoAnne remembers her husband just offering, "Why don't I stay home?" Her knee-jerk reaction was to question the idea. She was afraid it might be emasculating, and she didn't want him to go through what she saw many stay-at-home moms at the time suffered from—a loss of identity.

As a way to circumvent that potential issue, they threw together a little business deal. "I said to him, 'Look, let's do this on a quarter by quarter basis. Every quarter, we're going to go out and have dinner and talk about how you feel about being a stay-at-home parent. You can opt-out at any time.' I always wanted to make it optional for him so he didn't feel like he was stuck." They outlined what the fallback plan would be should he decide to go back to work. She even included benefits in their contractual agreement. "The other deal we struck was I told him three weeks of vacation a year, wherever you want to go."

THE GOLDEN RULE OF PARTNERSHIP

"We have a very unconventional marriage for the '90s. This was before Oprah even talked about stay-at-home dads!" JoAnne was very intentional about coming up with an arrangement that was fair to her husband. "I thought it was super important. I wanted him to feel valued and so I treated him the way I would want to be treated if I were the stay-at-home parent." She was adamant that she wanted him to have his own sense of identity and time to dedicate to his own hobbies, socialize with friends, and completely remove himself from the home environment when he needed to. "A lot of people thought my husband was so spoiled, which I thought was ridiculous because I was just treating him with the respect I would have wanted in the same situation. I don't think men actually think about it like this when they have a stay-at-home wife." For JoAnne, it was all about the Golden Rule!

By giving him the chance to opt-out at any time, JoAnne felt their contract wouldn't create the pressure zone that often leads to unhappiness in many marriages. They outlined Option B, which was to get a full-time nanny. They even went so far as to determine Option C, which entailed him going back to work part-time. Getting together once a quarter to talk about their arrangement turned into conversations about just how well their kids were doing. JoAnne recounted one such conversation, "We discovered that through talking about all of the things they were doing and accomplishing that our kids were truly thriving! It was because of this agreement we made. At that point, it was clear we made the right decision." JoAnne and her husband went out to a special dinner every quarter for ten years to discuss how he felt about staying at home. The arrangement worked so well that other parents even recognized the unique benefits of their contract!

IN IT TOGETHER

While her husband stayed at home, he wasn't the one doing all the chores! "All of the neighborhood kids were always over at our house. I swear we never had less than ten people at our dinner table every night." The cost of hanging out at the Kennedy household was pulling your weight in chores. "I think our kids were pretty embarrassed by us making other kids clean the house. Our thought process was if we're going to act as a community and a family, then everybody gets to participate in the good of Dad's cooking and the mundane of folding laundry."

With a whole bunch of kids always over at the house, the chores went by quickly. They learned everything from how to fold laundry to cleaning toilets to washing the floor... by hand! It paid off though. One day, JoAnne got a call from one of the neighborhood moms. The woman had just injured her back and couldn't do anything around the house—not even tie her own shoes. Up until that point, that mom had done everything around the house for her boys. Now that she was out of commission, she thought they were in for trouble. The woman called JoAnne to thank her because she caught her son cleaning up the kitchen, wiping down the counter, and cleaning the floors. She said to JoAnne, "I never taught him how to do these things. He must have learned them over at your house. Thank you!" It was a win-win situation for everyone!

FAMILY FIRST

JoAnne rose through the ranks early and was very ambitious in her career. She laughed, thinking back on her trajectory pre-kids, "Anyone who knew me at that time thought I would never have kids. I was too ambitious.

Then when I had four, they told me I was crazy!" Early in the young mom season of her career, JoAnne made a conscious choice to be there for her kids. She made every single outing and field trip from preschool through elementary school for all four of her kids. "My husband and I chaperoned them all. For organizations that I was leading, I would be very direct with them and say, 'Today, from 9 AM to 1 PM, I'm taking my preschooler to the trout farm.'"

By being direct in her communication and open about her work schedule, her actions also gave permission for other parents to do the same. After those excursions, JoAnne might log back on in the evening but she showed up when it counted and made memories with her family. She had the courage and conviction to tell her employer what her needs were as an employee. Her work ethic made up for her time out of the office. To JoAnne, "It's all about balance and prioritization in advance and having the courage to draw those boundaries for yourself."

As a leader, she supports and appreciates when the mothers on her team take time to go on field trips. "I am so encouraging and very genuine when I tell them I want them to have those experiences with their kids. I did, and I wouldn't trade those memories for the world!"

Pearls of Wisdom:

- Be active and intentional in how you maintain and build relationships. Christine had to put herself out there and prioritize her time in order to create an incredible neighborhood community for her and her family. The risk is worth the reward!

- True partnership boils down to three things: enjoying your time with your significant other, prioritizing their happiness, and seeing the value in everything they do. Suzanne works hard every day to maintain the partnership she has built with her husband of thirty-four years and it shows.

- The Golden Rule of Partnership: Treat your partner how you would want to be treated in any given situation. Open communication and appreciation are key to creating a positive, working relationship. For stay-at-home parents, establish your own contract! Together, decide what terms and conditions apply to maintain a healthy sense of individual identity and perspective.

Chapter 7

Making Your Community VIP

"To protect your energy:
It's okay to cancel a commitment.
It's okay to not answer a call.
It's okay to change your mind.
It's okay to want to be alone.
It's okay to take a day off.
It's okay to do nothing.
It's okay to speak up.
It's okay to let go."

—LORI DESCHENE[10]

---

10 Deschene, Lori. "To Protect Your Energy". *Tiny Buddha*, 2019.

The two most important resources you have are your energy and time. It is important to invest both wisely. Often the people we surround ourselves with impact both of those resources. Choosing to spend time with your friends and family uses up precious time. Whether they project a positive or negative outlook on life affects your fragile energy.

For that reason, it is important to carefully curate the people you invest your time in. Their optimism or pessimism will inevitably impact your energy levels—the Law of Attraction in action. Surrounding yourself with positive individuals will help you be more positive. Whereas, if you choose to expend your energy spending time with negative individuals, you will feel drained and exhausted with your life and the world around you.

This is why we must only admit VIP members into our inner circle—people full of Vitally Important Positivity. Colleen Richey and Kalee Tyson are prime examples of building deep relationships with people who share similar interests and values. They do it thoughtfully and recycle on an as-needed basis.

INTENTION IS EVERYTHING

Meet Colleen Richey, a networker by nature and pursuer of awesome people.

In her life, Colleen has always made it a point to surround herself with women who were putting out positive energy into the world and on a similar path to her own. While she was in college, she gravitated toward joining a sorority with the motto "women building strong girls," and she has continued to pay that sentiment forward throughout her life. She even created a mentor program at that same institution to create a safe space for young women to find and foster those VIP relationships.

YOUR A-LIST

She jokes with a friend that she has an A-List of friends in her life. Her A-List is where Colleen chooses to invest her time. "I seek out those on that A-List intentionally." In curating a community of women who embody VIP, the relationships are mutually important and energizing. Each person can learn, grow, and be inspired by the others. There is symbiosis to VIP communities whereas other friend groups can be riddled with drama and toxic relationships. Colleen aims to build relationships filled with VIP energy.

Sometimes, you find yourself down the rabbit hole, hanging around people who stray from your values. "I try very hard to not be a catty woman and make the women around me better. If I go out for an evening with a group and they are putting down other people or gossiping, there is a very high probability that I'm going to Irish-exit out of that group. I want to be a part of group dynamics that add life, versus situations like those that I believe pull the life out of you."

In those moments, it is important to bring yourself back to center and remember who you are and what values guide you. Get out of friendships that don't support you in the ways you need them to. You have to remind yourself of your purpose when others are dragging you down to their level. Colleen shared how she practices this, "I tell myself firmly that this is not who I am. I am out here to make people better." By trusting her values, Colleen is able to intentionally make time to invest in those friendships that are full of VIP energy.

TRAIN YOURSELF TO FIND VIP PEOPLE

Colleen is a student of relationships. By nature, she is an avid networker, so in her pursuit of her A-List, she learned over time what to look for when she runs across new and interesting people. "You can meet them anywhere!" She told me the story of a sorority sister of hers, Laurie Black, as an example of serendipitous timing.

The two women were in the same Gamma Phi house in college; however, their friendship didn't blossom until years later. Laurie was a year older and the two never really interacted. It was through their sons' shared baseball team that they learned how much they had in common. Both were working moms. Both had a passion for mentoring the next generation. Both were committed to surrounding themselves with high-quality, VIP people.

Be very intentional. Colleen does not put up with drama for a reason, as it doesn't serve to cultivate VIP communities. Hang out with women who are out to build each other up and make each other better.

THE WORLD NEEDS MORE IRONWOMEN

World, meet Kalee Tyson. All-Star recruiter at Slalom Consulting, talented Ironman athlete, loving wife, and adoring dog mom of Wilson, the cutest corgi ever.

Swimming 2.4 miles. Biking 112 miles. Running a 26.2-mile marathon. One right after the other immediately. No break. This is the reality of the legendary Ironman

Triathlon race. It is the hardest single-day endurance race in the entire world. It requires *at least* six months of intense training before you can even think about attempting the real thing.

When I looked up what it takes to compete in the Ironman race, an article from *The Telegraph* popped up entitled "10 Things You Need To Know About Ironman Triathlons.[11]" What I only realized after reading through the entire article was that it was labeled under "Men" then "Active" categories on the website. It was published in 2015 by a man for men. Yet the language in the article is not gender-specific. It was hard for me to conceptualize that just by two simple classifications of category, sexism showed through.

A COMPETITIVE HEART

Kalee is the definition of a competitor. When we were talking about how she got into endurance sports, Kalee told me her origin story that she could trace back all the way to her college days at the University of Washington.

"It's kind of embarrassing why I got into running." She chuckled a bit as she spoke. "So I played soccer growing

---

11   Anderson, Stuart. "10 Things You Need To Know About Ironman Triathlons". *Telegraph.Co.Uk*, 2015.

up and I tore my ACL when I was seventeen, which effectively stopped my athletic endeavors. When I went to college, I was just working out at the IMA [University of Washington's student gym] and being a normal person. However, I actually started running because I was competing internally with other sorority girls on the treadmill. It sounds weird, I know." She stuck to the treadmill to protect her knee at first but her competitive heart pushed Kalee to outrun those around her. She was motivated to... stride... for more (does this count as a running pun?).

Kalee traded in the elliptical for running indoors. From there, she pushed herself to progress. She moved slowly at first from indoor running to outdoor running, which then snowballed into "marathons just kind of by progression."

BECOMING AN IRONWOMAN

Kalee seems to be operating in overdrive to accomplish the goals she sets for herself. When her internal drive wavers, what keeps her motivated to continue training toward her goal?

If your answer was *community,* then you are correct! Her progression from amateur elliptical enthusiast to successful conqueror of marathons was built on many 5ks, 10ks, and half marathons before she got her first marathon experience. Kalee was able to build a community of motivated runners along that journey who collectively pushed each other to achieve that first milestone: finishing a marathon. Finding this community helped Kalee expand her love of running and exposed her to others who were compelled by inner competitive fire to succeed athletically.

A couple of her new running friends decided they were going to compete in a triathlon. Kalee's competitive heart took over when she heard this, that voice in her head shouted, "They are not better athletes than me. If they can do it, then I can do it!" The idea of friendly competition and moving up the ladder in a physical test of the endurance was too sweet to pass up. "So I just did it!"

Kalee could be a Nike commercial. She decides she wants to tackle a new challenge and just does it!

SACRIFICE FOR THE SAKE OF GROWTH

When this transition to triathlon came into her life, Kalee was in a self-proclaimed rut. "I think I was going through an interesting point in life personally. I just wanted something new. I think when you transition out of school, specifically, you go through this interesting phase of starting to grow up. This might sound bad but you're not wanting to party all the time and you want to figure out where you're going. For me, I was professionally progressing, but as an individual, my growth was stagnant. The one thing I could control on an individual level was athletics."

As she built out her training schedule, Kalee actively made the choice to dedicate a large majority of her free time to realize this goal. It meant she had to miss some happy hours and events with friends. Some of them didn't care to pause and understand her choices. Instead, they harped on her for not spending enough time with them.

"I had to give those people up. It was a sacrifice for me, definitely, but I had grown out of that phase of my life and those people." Kalee chose to recycle some of her more party-focused friends for the sake of her own personal sanity. It was necessary to surround herself with VIP individuals who supported her goals. A supportive VIP community was the only way she was going to get there.

When Kalee commits herself to something, she doesn't half-ass it. Instead of signing up for a shorter course to build-up to the holy grail of triathlon races, she signed up for Ironman. Her husband signed up in solidarity. "We just went for it."

AWESOME COACHING MAKES A DIFFERENCE
What happens when you decide you want to level-up?

For Kalee, the accountability of her community was motivating, but it wasn't the answer for measuring her progress and pushing her limits. To conquer the next steps on her journey, she needed outside help. It was time to find a coach.

"I think when you're having to push yourself, athletically, it's always so helpful to have somebody to lean on from an emotional standpoint. You need a third party to tell you to keep going, to encourage you, and to help you hone your craft. Having a coach in the triathlon space for me was a game-changer." In Kalee's experience, you don't know your athletic limits until someone forces you to keep going because they see your potential and know your goals. Last year, 2018, was Kalee's first year really leveling-up in the sport and becoming a lot more competitive. You can't fathom how much you are capable of until you find that level of support. "In your head, you think you've hit your limit and then, with a little help, you realize that you're truly only halfway there."

Pursuing this essential coaching component is not limited to Kalee's success in her athletic training. It has also manifested in how she has grown professionally.

Kalee's former boss, Maryana, gave her the kind of professional coaching she needed to level up in her career. She truly believes that when someone who has faith in you challenges you to try something new or accomplish a goal outside of your proverbial wheelhouse, the specific positive encouragement motivates the individual to reach new heights. "I never would have thought I could output as much work as I've been producing and manage one of the higher producing teams in the business and still be training at the level that I am. It was my old boss, Maryana, who told me 'you can totally do that; you got this,' and helped me to take on more and more over time. You just have to act."

Kalee reflected on her growth at Slalom over the past four years. "It's wild to look back to when I first started my career. What I thought was a hard day back then is one-eighth of a typical day for me now. It's just too funny. I didn't even know what busy truly meant."

INTEGRATING ALL ASPECTS OF LIFE TO BUILD A FUTURE

How does Kalee cope with all of the craziness of today?

Work-Life Integration. How tech-y is that! The different theories out there popularly deemed "Work-Life Balance" and "Work-Life Harmony," the term coined by Amazon, are flawed. There's always a little bit of imbalance. It is rare for work and personal life to be in perfect harmony. Kalee was adamant that though she strives to practice Work-Life Integration, her life is not perfect. "There are weeks where I am very fatigued, and my brain is not performing at top-notch. There's no such thing as perfect balance. However, I still strive for the best balance or best integration."

So what API (tech people... see what I did there) or practice does Kalee exercise to create this Work-Life Integration for herself? What is her secret sauce?

Drum roll, please... *Sleep!* Kalee gets eight hours of sleep a night. "It's a non-negotiable for me." Her personal take on sleep is that people generally take it for granted. As I write this is, it 2 AM and I know full well that I need to get up at 7 AM. Looks like I need to start practicing Kalee's secret! If she doesn't get enough sleep, as an athlete, it inhibits her ability to train. As a professional, if she doesn't get all eight hours in, then her brain refuses to function at top speed. Those are the two things she cares most about. Prioritizing sleep keeps her on her game.

It's something most people overlook. We hear stories of executives who operate on four hours of sleep a night and are able to conquer the world. That may work for them, but for the normal human, it is nearly impossible to excel if you aren't resting and recharging at night. "My sister used to sleep five hours a night because she was doing too many things and hit a breaking point. Recently, she is sleeping eight hours a night and feels like a whole new human. It's a weird concept but it's powerful."

IRONCLAD GOALS

As goal-oriented as Kalee is, it would be remiss if I didn't ask her what's next on her "To Crush" list. She had two focuses:

1. Bringing little kiddos into the world
2. Qualifying for Kona

Speaking to her first goal, she set a timeline—hopefully, within the next three years. She is fully on board with decreasing her triathlon lifestyle in small ways to work toward building an "integration" where those three elements of her life—work, Ironman, and children—can work together to build a wonderfully full life. Kalee has observed the community of brand-new mamas on her team at Slalom, listening to their stories for nuggets of wisdom to apply to her own soon-to-be working-mom life. With that support system already in place, Kalee is excited to see what motherhood will bring.

In the world of Ironman, Kona is akin to Mount Olympus for the Greeks. It is the pinnacle of the sport. To qualify, it takes a special combination of speed, work ethic, and luck. In order to qualify for the World Championship of Ironman held in Kona, Hawaii, a triathlete must first have a great day. According to Kalee, Ironman doesn't always go well. When you have ten to fifteen-hour days, there is a huge mental component required to be successful. Not only must they race well as an individual, but the triathlete must also outperform other racers at the qualifier as well. This sounds like a given, yet you never know who will show up on race day. Sometimes, you can get lucky with the ability level of people you race against. Kalee hopes to qualify within the next ten years. By 2030, she hopes to have competed amongst the best in the world.

Goals are great. They keep people motivated to grow and work toward something. In each of Kalee's two goals, there are micro-goals she will accomplish along the way.

This creates a dynamic path. As each mini-win comes, there are new variables and elements to consider. Having a well-integrated life is all well and good, but if that life requires some additional elements, it is important to be open and embrace the required change.

Kalee is willing to sacrifice commitment to the sport she loves in order to create a family. In this new season of her life, Kalee's work-life-athletics integration will look different. Being willing to make adjustments is how one is able to build out the best operating version of the life they want to live.

Pearls of Wisdom:
- Be intentional about seeking out and incorporating VIP members into your A-List. When you feel yourself straying from your values, check in with your energy and take a close look at who you spend your time with.
- Recycling is not only good for the environment; it is also good for your mental health. If a friend is no longer a positive force in your life or supporting your goals, then they do not deserve your time or energy.

Chapter 8

Impact of Community

"It takes a village.[12]*"*

This highly-quoted adage originates from an African proverb communicating the importance of the collective support of community. Life can be a real heavy-weight hitter. You get knocked to the ground and sometimes you can't get back up on your own. Having a support system in place and learning how to lean on them when you need it most is a difficult skill, yet one that can make all the difference when life throws a left hook.

---

12   Goldberg, Joel. "It Takes A Village To Determine The Origins Of An African Proverb". *Npr.Org,* 2016.

WHEN TRAGEDY STRIKES

THE FINANCIAL ADVISOR IN FINANCIAL RUIN

Meet Jane (name has been changed). Mom, financial advisor, and Superwoman.

In 2008, Jane suffered through more than just the crash of the stock market. She knew something was wrong with her marriage and their finances but could not figure out what exactly was going on. Her marriage wasn't perfect, but she was at a loss about the cause of their problems until one evening in August. That night, she learned her husband, who doubled as the bookkeeper for her business, had secretly been syphoning off money from her business and their household resources to fund his secret addiction. This realization hit her like a truck. She was completely in shock both by the addiction and by the significant amount of money he had spent over the many years they were married.

Prior to that night, several indicators foreshadowed this turn of events in her marriage. Registered mail showed up to her house from the IRS informing her that taxes she'd written a check for and mailed in from two years prior were due. Her banker uncovered several transfers out of Jane's business account into a separate account her husband held with another bank. At this point, her banker felt the financial responsibility to tell Jane what she found. Jane recalled the exchange in her banker's office, "She told me frankly, 'There's something terribly wrong here. You make plenty of money but I can't account for $75,000 of it in the past year. How is your marriage?' My response was, 'Well, I know it's not what I thought it would be, but we have a child, and I've made a commitment for life.'"

However, the situation hit a boiling point when she discovered he hadn't paid a portion of their taxes. Financially, he decimated their family as a result of his online addictions, forcing Jane and her business into significant financial pressure and wedged Jane between a rock and a hard place. Luckily, the wealth management practice she'd built over the last nineteen years was thriving. Many of her colleagues, including her business partner, mentor, and close personal friend were all there to support her during this traumatic time in her life. For her own safety and to protect her daughter, Jane chose to leave her husband and fortunately, she had the financial means to do so. She was so grateful then and continues to recognize how important it is to have financial freedom and be aware and know what is going on with your finances in your marriage, regardless of who is earning the money. Many women she knew at the time she was going through this were not able to leave their situations because they did not have the financial wherewithal to do so.

But wait... there's more. One of Jane's closest friends and colleagues died of brain cancer earlier that same year. Two weeks after her friend lost her battle with brain cancer, that same friend's husband succumbed to pancreatic cancer, leaving behind two high-school-age girls. To top it all off, Jane's mother had a heart attack and was in the hospital. Jane reflects on the cataclysmic tragedy that hit in 2008: "It was a mess. I was a mess. Everyone was so focused on the stock market crash, but I had so many other problems to worry about it hardly even registered. In 2008, the stock market was the least of my problems!"

In this season of her life, Jane could think of little other than simply surviving. "I was literally off the grid for the better part of a year. Without my team backing me up and my business partner stepping in to help, along with our managing partner and my parents, the outcome would have been very different." Jane's family was all in and ready to fill the gaps. "My family was here for us 110% and because of that, I didn't have to worry that my daughter was okay. She would go over to my sister's after school so I could get work done." Jane feels truly blessed for the freedom and flexibility her career offers in addition to the invaluable support system that rallied around her during that painful period of her life.

Eventually, Jane got to a level of financial stability that afforded her the bandwidth to hire a nanny. Her daughter, who has a very keen sense of people's personalities, found her soon-to-be nanny out at a restaurant. She was Jane and her daughter's server. "She leaned over to me and said, 'Mom, I think she would make a great nanny!' I said, 'Really?' I watched her as she solved problems, her positive attitude, and her smiling face as the stress of the busy lunch hour challenged her, and I agreed to ask her about her interest and if she had any experience!" Jane got the woman's phone number and discovered she really needed medical insurance and full-time employment. The two worked out a deal. Jane needed more administrative help in her office so she hired her to come into the office in the morning and work part-time to get the benefits she needed. When school got out, she would then flip into nanny mode! "To this day, she is one of my top performers on our team, having been promoted many times over the years, now becoming an advisor herself! It became obvious to me to hire her full time. I gave her the option; office or nanny? She, of course, wanted the office! That one decision has changed the entire trajectory of her life forever! She's incredible!" The one caveat was she had to break the news to Jane's daughter that her favorite nanny would be leaving...

Jane and her daughter constructed a new family unit. One that was built on the support and love of their family and greater community. "She grew up in my business with me," Jane said of her daughter. "She's quite the saleswoman and one day might even take over my practice. She's seen how I financially help and empower women and is proud of me. That is the biggest reward for all of the sacrifices we have had to make." Jane is passionate about her career as a Wealth Management Advisor; it's given her the intangibles she never would have expected—control of her own destiny, colleagues who are now lifelong family, and the means to empower other women!

SURGICAL SCARES
Meet Julie Johns.

The bad news was delivered with the birth of her first son. He was diagnosed with a heart defect straight out of the gate and within the first eight hours of his life was whisked off to Seattle Children's Hospital. Each year, Julie's son goes back multiple times for regular testing. The Johns have such a deep appreciation for the work that Seattle Children's Hospital does that they founded a guild to help offset the expense of uncompensated care. No child is turned away at this premier pediatric hospital. They felt fortunate to have Children's in their backyard and hoped to offset the expense for the hospital caring for uninsured children who suffer from similar care needs.

At age fourteen, the doctors told Julie her son needed open-heart surgery. The reality of the situation was so overwhelming that she had a hard time processing what was happening in advance of the surgery. "I just worked up until starter day. It helped me to stay calm and took my mind off of it. We had a phenomenal support system of my family, my husband's family, and our close friends, as well as my team at Microsoft." While Julie's family waited at the hospital, those wonderful people brought her family food and hung out, helping to keep morale high and the focus on healing. Julie's family felt blessed to receive top-quality care from Seattle Children's. "Just thinking about other families who don't have insurance to cover that kind of procedure. I was with Microsoft at the time so I had outstanding benefits. It was a $280,000 surgery, and I think I paid like 2,500 bucks out of pocket." The reason her family started the guild rang even truer after this surgery.

After the open-heart surgery, while her son was recovering, Julie took five weeks off of work to focus on her family. Microsoft was understanding of her situation, allowing her the space to prioritize her family. This surgical scare put everything into perspective for Julie. One of her old managers, who she still remains friends with to this day, and Julie lightheartedly reframed the significance of their jobs by saying, "We aren't saving babies." The work they do is valuable, and it is important to get it all done, yet Julie jokes, "But no one's going to lose their life if I don't show up to work or if I take an extra day off." Taking five weeks off to take care of her baby was what was important to her during that turbulent time in her family's life. Her eldest son just celebrated his sixteenth birthday.

"My son's open-heart surgery put a lot of things into perspective for me. I know now what is going to make the sky fall and what isn't." Mentally assigning and shifting the value placed on the pieces of your life allows you to understand what "makes the sky fall" and prioritize as necessary.

At work, Julie scrapes the easy tasks off the top. If it takes her thirty seconds, she gets it out of the way. However, when a meteor project hits—you know, those big one that make an impact—she will strategically block out time on her calendar to ensure she can get it done. "Aside from understanding how your role impacts your company, it's also important to understand how your choices will impact your family." Julie made a deal with her kids. If it is important to her kiddos that she go to their Valentine's Day party at school or chaperone a field trip, they have to voice it.

"Okay, so I'm not the PTA mom. I love my children dearly and anything they really want me to do, I am one hundred percent in every day of the week." Her youngest son is a ten-year-old stud baseball player. It is his absolute favorite thing and during the season, there are weeks where he has up to three games starting at 5 PM, an hour from where Julie works. To show up for her son, on those three days, she leaves work at 3:30 to get home and get him to the field on time. "I prioritize it because I know it's important to him, and I personally enjoy it. Then when I get home, I log back on and see if there are any emergencies that have transpired and address those at that time."

A terribly scary situation as a parent turned into a positive. Not only did her eldest son recover, but she was also given the gift of perspective and a bar against which to measure when it comes to investing time and emotional energy.

HARD-FOUGHT BATTLES

Meet Mychele Riddick. Mother. Career AT&T employee. All around positive person.

As she would describe it, nine years ago she had the perfect life. "I have my perfect, handsome husband. I have my two beautiful little girls that I talk about all the time. I have a good job at AT&T. Then, when we turned fifty, my husband went in and had a colonoscopy. The results came back that he had stage-four colon cancer." Mychele's husband fought hard for three and a half years following his diagnosis but ultimately lost his battle with colon cancer. Mychele found herself as a single parent to twelve and fifteen-year-old girls trying to navigate this new season of her life in the wake of tragedy.

"This is when AT&T turned into a family for me." She described how her colleagues from across the country offered their support in incredible ways. While her husband was in the trenches of his fight doing chemo, a peer from an East Coast office reached out, sending articles and recipes that helped her own mother during her experience with colon cancer. Another colleague directed Mychele toward insurance resources supported by AT&T that would allow for a second opinion at no charge. "My team gave me all the support and as much time as I needed to take my husband to chemo sessions, take time off during his surgeries. Whatever I needed, they helped make happen. It didn't matter what the handbook policy said."

She received condolence letters from direct reports to the CEO on down to those in her Sacramento office. Peers flew out all the way from Chicago and North Carolina to attend her husband's funeral. "That made me feel like my kids are their kids, too. They look after them. They support them in any way they can. They ask about them, and it makes me want to get up and work for this company every day. Couldn't do it without a village. Couldn't do it without their support."

The biggest example of how her colleagues supported her children was following the death of their dad, her whole office banded together and created college savings accounts for both daughters. "They put together scholarships and gathered enough money together to open two Roth IRA accounts for my girls. It is interesting to reflect on how that money is being used right now. My youngest daughter is leaving for college in the fall. It really is a full-circle moment."

Reflecting back now, Mychele believes that this tragic situation and the support she received from those around her has shown her the type of person she wants to be. "I learned to be a better person. I learned how to be more empathetic because the community around me was so mind-blowingly amazing when I was going through a really dark time." When describing her community, Mychele was adamant their support was beyond her wildest dreams and helped her to adapt to her new circumstances in ways that changed her outlook on life.

One such change came from a speech given by former VP at AT&T and current CEO for the Dallas Mavericks. As a mom, Cynthia described how she goes about prioritizing events in her family. Mychele explained to me Cynthia's decision-making philosophy, "Sometimes in life, you have crystal balls, and you have rubber balls. There's going to be some events in your child's life that you're just not going to be able to make. You may not be able to sit home and have dinner every day at five o'clock. You may not make it to a softball game. But it is vitally important to have that communication with your family and you have to understand what is precious to them. So, a rubber ball example is pick up from soccer practice on Tuesday night. A crystal ball is going to the championship game. That crystal ball is going to break; you can't put those pieces back together. The rubber ball, on the other hand, will bound back to you; it is recoverable." When Mychele identifies those "crystal ball" moments in her own life, she lights up a metaphorical neon glowing *closed* sign to set the expectation that she is not available to her company. Setting those boundaries and openly communicating priorities with loved ones makes the difference between shattering a crystal ball and bouncing a rubber one.

LEARNING HOW TO ASK FOR HELP

Not all help comes in the wake of hardship. Sometimes, it can be difficult to ask for help when you need it most. One major season of life that this comes into play, for women especially, is when cute little babies come into the world. They are so freaking adorable and yet they turn your life upside-down.

STEP 1: Understand You are Not an Island

Meet Laurel Duquette. Sales Manager at Snapchat. Wife. New Momma.

For Laurel Duquette to even have a thirty-minute interview with me, she needed to go to her parents' house down the street so they could feed and watch her three-month-old son. Her house is currently filled with construction workers during a remodel and she needed thirty uninterrupted minutes to make it happen. "I was stressed with the million people at our house and feeding my son so I called up my parents, and I think they heard the strain in my voice when I asked, 'Can I come over,' but nonetheless, I was able to make it happen!"

She wasn't always great at asking for help. Laurel recalls after having her first child, "I wanted so desperately to try and figure it out for myself. I also struggled with a lot of anxiety probably in the form of postpartum. Asking for that help was really tough for me." It took a while for her to get comfortable with the idea that she needed to wave the white flag and lean on those around her. Laurel found support from new mom groups and communities that really helped her understand that she was not an island in her experience. In this season of her life, she didn't have to have it all together all the time and those groups helped her internalize that message. "You think you're in bad shape, and you get there, and you realize you're all in the same boat. It puts things into perspective. Whereas previously I felt like I was in a different world that no one could understand or relate to."

Now Laurel has learned little tips and tricks to prevent that feeling all centered around effective communication. "The concept it takes a village is so true. I think a lot of that starts at home with your husband or partner and being really clear about expectations about what's important to you both personally and professionally."

Laurel gives her husband a lot of credit for being a less traditional partner. "I would say our roles are very blended. He cleans and goes to the grocery store and helps with drop off. It's all about communication." Laurel also lives right near family. So when she needed thirty minutes to herself to do this interview she was able to head over to her parents at a moment's notice. Her sister also has two kids, so in surrounding herself with those who prioritize family, Laurel feels it keeps her grounded.

Last, but certainly not least, in the support system is their nanny! "Sometimes, you hear women deliver keynotes or post on social media about their success, and it's not often enough they recognize and honor these people that help raise their kids and follow their rules and guidelines. She truly is part of the family, and I can't say enough about my nanny and the impact she's had on our ability to work and raise grounded kids and take care of things." It is so important to recognize the people who support you in your life. It's good karmic energy.

STEP 2: Assemble Your Army

There are also superwomen like former Executive Vice President at Nordstrom, Laurie Black.

This woman only missed one school event ever in her sons' lives because a volcano erupted in Alaska and her flight physically wasn't able to take off safely. She did it through effective communication as well as building a small army of well-trained helpers.

At one point early on in her merchandising career, one of the VPs of Nordstrom at the time gave Laurie some invaluable advice. He told her to not make the mistake he had in missing all of his kids' stuff. In her role, she was on a plane every week traveling to different stores across the nation for store openings, celebrity events, and more. It was a job that took her away from her family. That nugget of advice really hit home with Laurie, and she set out to find a way to be there for her kids and all of their sports games, preschool events, teacher conferences, etc. "We were held accountable for getting our work done for sure. But it wasn't like we had to be in the office every day from 8 AM to 5 PM. We just needed to get our jobs done, didn't matter when or how we did it."

In her thirty-five-year career at Nordstrom, Laurie only missed one of her son's events—a pre-school performance. She was working up in Alaska when the volcano erupted. Laurie's flight was immediately canceled, and she physically didn't have a way to get back to Seattle. Barring natural disaster, Laurie was at all important events for her kids. She set the expectation with her team and management to make sure that everyone was on the same page.

Laurie distinctly remembers an event that was scheduled for a Saturday at the Bellevue location. She had an entire team dedicated to the event. Her boss at the time, Pete Nordstrom, asked Laurie if she would be there, and she responded honestly that she would not be there because her son had a championship ski race. He was confused and pushed a little harder. However, his insistence didn't faze Laurie. She laughs in memory of her response to Pete. "I told him that it wasn't crucial for me to be there when I had a whole team of people running the event and, quite frankly, I wanted to be at my son's ski race!" Laurie remembers walking out of his office and thinking for a split second she might get fired for her flip comment. After that interaction, her manager understood her boundaries and never brought it up again. Now that work was onboard, it was time to assemble the army to make it all happen.

Her army started with the perfect co-general. Laurie's husband enjoyed filling in when she wasn't around. "He is really good at it, but he also enjoys it. That's the difference. Not all men like playing that role." Laurie has girlfriends whose husbands fall into the latter category.

Their fix is to up their babysitter's hours or hire on a full-time nanny. Fortunately for Laurie, she had an endless source of high-quality babysitters ready to be trained and put to work. Throughout her career, Laurie has maintained involvement with her college sorority acting as Rush Advisor for more than fifteen years. Her sustained relationship with the house meant she could easily find a high-quality babysitter she could trust.

"I think it honestly made my sons better people being surrounded by such wonderful young women. Our UW babysitters were so entrenched in our lives they became a part of the family. I'm still on a texting basis with a lot of them. One just had a baby. Another just got married. It's really fun to see how they've blossomed." When her babysitters were over, they knew her house backward and forward. She was a master delegator, so she was able to divide up tasks like stuffing Christmas card envelopes and other small, time-consuming tasks to her babysitters in order to take more off of her own plate.

By training her army to work as efficiently as she would, Laurie was able to cover more ground and spend her quality time with her family.

Pearls of Wisdom:

- Falling apart is okay! Let the people around you step in and take care of you when you need it. Life punches hard. Julie Prince learned how to punch back only after her team helped her back to her feet.
- A health scare can give you a healthy dose of perspective on what is truly important in your life. Julie Johns learned to roll with the punches at work because she understands the role she plays in her work and how that relates to her first priority—her family.
- Loss is tragic. Even the hardest fought battles can be lost. The silver lining for Mychele came in the form of a new work family who loved and cared for her daughters more than she ever hoped!
- Learn that it is okay to ask for help when you need it! You need to know you cannot operate as an island and that assembling an army is the best chance you have at success.

Part Three

Eyes on the Prize

Chapter 9

Risk Takers & Change Makers

I want to show you that adversity is not crippling. It is what lines the rocky road to resilience! Here are two incredible women who have survived, thrived, and paved the way for the women after them. As Nelson Mandela said, "Education is the most powerful weapon which you can use to change the world.[13]"

DARE TO BE MORE

Meet Valerie Palmer. Asylee (seeker of asylum), mother, neurological disease researcher, instructor of neurology, and mentor.

13　"Nelson Mandela." In *Oxford Essential Quotations*, edited by Ratcliffe, Susan. Oxford University Press.

This woman doesn't take no for an answer. Her entire mission is to form multi-disciplinary cross-collaborative groups that work together to solve public health issues, study causes of disease and prevent them. Valerie's source of inspiration? Apartheid and her genetic makeup.

GROWING UP UNDER APARTHEID

Valerie grew up in a mixed-race community in Kwa-Zulu (formally Zululand) Natal, South Africa during the Apartheid era. The laws instituted by the government during this time sought to separate and create tension among different racial groups. During Valerie's time in South Africa, a colored bar system divided South Africans into four groups: European, Asians, Mixed-Race, and Indigenous. Banks, hospitals, schools, beaches, post offices, and other public locations were separated into four sections for each group to use. There was no inter-mingling and animosity for other groups ran high at the time.

Her formative years under the oppressive regime shaped her experiences and how she processes the world. Spending her childhood in South Africa, Valerie faced many problems. Yet she credits her success today to what those early experiences taught her. Valerie shared, "Because I am the oldest girl in my family, I had the difficult task of having to take care of my four brothers and sister. My younger brothers were terrors and a handful. Around nine or ten years of age, I was left in charge of managing the farm, caring for my brothers and sister as well as the sick and injured in the community. I was like a mother and father for my siblings and a little doctor for the community and farm animals. So that built some very good strength in me." At the time, Valerie didn't know just how much she would rely on her strength later in life.

Another challenge she faced was being force-fed propaganda that told Valerie she was inferior because of her genetics. Logically, this never made sense to Valerie, and as a teenager, she decided to push back and fight against the idea that the color of her skin set limits on what she could accomplish in her life. Her father's involvement in the politics of South Africa and the government's push for separate development along with the call for equality piqued her interest. Valerie got involved with the Coloured Peoples Youth Labour Party of South Africa— where she traveled around the KwaZulu area speaking to local youth groups on the importance of education and why they needed to be recognized as equal citizens in South Africa.

Barely eleven years old, Valerie was chosen as the Secretary for the Coloured Peoples Youth Labour Party of

South Africa. "At seventeen, I was told by my father that he learned that the secret police were tracking me and that I may be in terrible danger. There were many individuals around me that were disappearing, and I never heard from them again. So I became very afraid that I may not live very much longer." The secret police were following Valerie around trying to understand what she was doing, why she was doing it, and to top it all off, the government refused to give her a passport for several years.

Fearing for her life, Valerie traveled to Britain where she sought asylum. She needed to survive to create change and thought she might be able to do a better job of changing South Africa from the outside. Her mission was to make an impact she could see. Valerie also shared, "I felt that I wanted to do more than just try to change the world of South Africa." After two years of waiting, Valerie was denied her request for asylum in Britain and knew returning to South Africa was a death sentence. Strategically, she pivoted to plan B and landed in the United States.

NEW LOCATION, NEW OPPORTUNITY

When she came to the United States, Valerie had a vision for the life she wanted for herself. "After growing up during Apartheid and being told I was inferior to others, I decided I would show them that I would be better than what they thought of me—that I would show them I could accomplish more. My whole thing is, when I'm being told that I cannot achieve anything, or can economically only do so much... that kind of talk just encourages me to do exactly the opposite. So when I was told I was never going to amount to anything, I decided not to listen." Valerie decided long before she moved to the United States that her passion and interests were in medical science. "When I left South Africa, at seventeen years old, I was headed toward opportunity. I was going to travel, I was going to do research, I was going to get involved in science, I was going to have a family, I would finally be free. Leaving meant I was going to do all sorts of things."

Like most big dreamers, Valerie started out in the Big Apple where she met her first husband and had her daughter. She then developed a successful business in New York City with a couple of partners, drawing on experiences from South Africa. A few years later, she founded a non-profit focused on the research of nutritional toxic diseases that affected the nervous system of the poorest populations internationally while she went back to school. "I wanted to know and learn about everything as much as possible." Focusing in on one topic or idea of study never made sense to Valerie. Her understanding of the world is from an interdisciplinary point of view. Narrowing her focus would mean lost learning opportunities. This worldview stems from her upbringing and her experiences on the family farm and the indigenous communities. Valerie grew up watching and helping people collaborate and form networks in her time in South Africa. She absolutely rejected the segregationist laws and ideologies attached to Apartheid and therein rejected looking at the world from a single viewpoint.

Valerie is adamant about an inter-disciplinary approach, especially in her work as a researcher and instructor. Her mantra is: "I believe in collaboration and cooperation of people, of all disciplines." With the help of a distinguished neuroscientist she met from the Albert Einstein College of Medicine in New York, Valerie set out to establish collaborative inter-professional research projects across the globe. They started in India then went to Bangladesh and Ethiopia, and on to study the cause of neurological diseases in some of the poorest parts of the world. Where the inter-disciplinary background of the group came into play was in gathering different data points and perspectives on the cause of the neurological disease in question and in determining how to go about putting infrastructure in place to prevent them from affecting so many impoverished people. Valerie elaborated on her purpose, "Studying causes of disease that affect populations in poor countries can give us clues to similar diseases internationally and lead to their prevention worldwide."

Of gathering people from different disciplines to come together and collaborate, Valerie remarked, "It is by no means an easy task, I will tell you that." She went on to describe that aside from the geographical challenges of getting everyone together in a room, "My biggest problem was that I was female and my second biggest problem was that I was a mixed-race South African." She ran into many men not appreciating being guided by a woman of color and had to tread carefully to get everyone on board. Valerie was able to align everyone on the cause and get them to buy into the idea of working together to address selected public health issues across the globe. She convinced governments and private institutions such as Canada (International Development Research Center), US (USAID, US Embassies, Ford & Rockefeller Foundation), and Britain (Save the Children and Band Aid) to participate. "Looking back on that time in my life, I was very bold." Valerie laughed in disbelief.

There were many wins both personally and professionally from her efforts. Valerie noted, "We organized several conferences in the UK, India, Bangladesh, Ethiopia, and US and published the proceedings of those gatherings. We traveled to many countries, including some remote areas, to conduct field research, videotape, and photograph neurodegenerative diseases. Often times presenting our findings a few days later at international conferences. The distinguished neuroscientist I teamed up with to accomplish all this became my husband in 2018, thirty years after we moved to Oregon where we continued our research work." The research Valerie referred to has been funded by several grants to do work in many impoverished parts of the world on a range of neurological diseases including Alzheimer's, Lathyrism, Konzo (paralyzing diseases caused by toxins in drought-resistant foods, grass pea and cassava respectively), dementia, Parkinson's, Lou Gehrig's disease, and Nodding Syndrome. She is still driven by the same core mission to make tangible impact across the world pursuing the field she loves. She is passionate about and has found incredible success in her pursuit of that dream.

ENTERING A WAR ZONE

The most exhilarating and dangerous research trip Valerie embarked on was to Papua province (formerly known as Irian Jaya) in West New Guinea. She ventured to the side controlled by Indonesia during a time of active conflict between the Indonesians and the indigenous Papuans. Valerie recalled why she was scared on that particular trip—aside from it being in an active war zone. "I was the only female together with a bunch of men rowing in a canoe going up a crocodile-infested river to a population that practiced head-hunting and cannibalism." How much worse could it get?

Valerie is adamant that her upbringing prepared her for just that moment. To get to school in South Africa, she would have to walk four miles along a grassy pathway with venomous snakes and scorpions. Along her route, Valerie had to cross two rivers filled with crocodiles. When she was in the canoe rowing upstream, the crocodiles were the least of her worries. "So those things didn't faze me as much," said Valerie of the crocs alongside her and her team in the river. "I was scared, don't get me wrong, but I was prepared for it. My background helped me talk myself through it and tell myself I would be okay and that I could deal with the situation." By tapping into her personal experiences, she was able to focus on the mission of the trip to help identify and document the possible cause of a serious health problem for the local people of Papua. The object of her research was a neurodegenerative disease identical to one she had studied in Guam and Japan. Valerie's formative years allowed her to think beyond herself in that situation because she knew she could handle whatever came her way.

DIVERSITY IS HER SUPERPOWER

Valerie hails from South Africa yet she is a product of many different cultures. She personally refers to herself as an "international" because taking the time to list off all of the cultures that contribute to her genetic makeup would take too long. The resulting effect is that she appeared local almost everywhere she has traveled to do field research. Her racial ambiguity was her secret weapon in establishing relationships with local communities. Valerie commented, "Across India, Thailand, and even in Japan, people tended to adopt me as though I was part of their culture."

She described numerous situations where the local population would get frustrated with her for not speaking their language. They would say to her, "You are Papuan or Okinawan! Why aren't you speaking our language? Why have you forgotten it?" Similar situations happened with local Indians requesting her to speak Hindi, as well as the Thai people she interacted with, being genuinely confused as to why she wouldn't speak Thai. From those exchanges, Valerie realized the power of her appearance. "What I understood from all those experiences was that my look could be from any of those countries. The way that all of the different ethnicities in my background combine make me appear to be one of those local populations."

In a way, the combination of all the different ethnicities in her background acted as a prism reflecting back the qualities that local peoples most resonated with. Valerie's racial ambiguity connected her deeply with the people she aimed to help in a way none of the European or American researchers on her team could replicate. Her diversity is literally her superpower and the foundation of her success. Not only that, all the hardships and all the difficulties she went through and experienced during the Apartheid era helped prepare her for the many different situations she encountered on her journey. Valerie explained, "I learned how to navigate and deal with tough situations as a result of my upbringing and these skills carried me through to follow my passion and my dreams."

LEARNING TO TAKE A BOW

When she is not studying neurological diseases across the globe, Valerie is changing her community through her work at the Oregon Health and Science University (OHSU). She has pioneered an inter-professional educational program that takes students (dental, pharmacy, nursing, nutrition, medicine, and more) outside of the university into local communities to work collaboratively in teams with disadvantaged people. They learn the value of teamwork across disciplines—the importance of culture and traditional practices of diverse populations—and they strive to include people in their own care in order to help themselves on a forward-going basis. In addition, Valerie had the privilege of developing and operating one of five centers charged with developing the gold standard for Toxicogenomic Research across the US at OHSU's Research Center on Occupational Environmental Toxicology (CROET). On interacting with her students, Valerie commented, "I also enjoyed training and mentoring students in laboratory and field research as well as in their masters and PhD studies."

For her efforts in creating an outstanding educational program at OHSU, Valerie was formally recognized at a national level by Encore. I asked her to take a moment and describe what that recognition felt like. "It's a feeling of total elation. I had no idea I could be recognized for this. I tend to be in the background rather than in the foreground. When it comes to recognition for things, I'm not really someone that seeks it out. But at the same time, it makes me feel very small because I feel like I haven't done that much. Overall, I'm very proud of the fact that students and communities have benefited from some of the stuff that I've done and appreciate the opportunity to work with the populations that I've worked with." As someone who generally operated in the background when it comes to awards and recognition, being the honoree was something Valerie had to learn to accept.

Her impact runs deep in the communities she has helped over the years. In addition to being recognized nationally and at OHSU, Valerie is also proud of the widely acknowledged collaborative research work she has done. She has been involved in producing many publications across various fields including but not limited to: a BBC documentary on neurodegenerative disease, videos on neurological disorders, and presented numerous papers and posters at international conferences. The breadth and depth of her knowledge are outstanding and is a valuable tool she uses to change the communities she strives to help!

The BBC documentary of ALS-PDC collaborative research can be found on Vimeo entitled "The Poison that Waits.[14]"

---

14   *Horizon.* "The Poison That Waits." Season 25, Episode 3. Valerie Palmer and colleagues. BBC, January 16, 1989. https://vimeo.com/1621281

REBEL WITH A CAUSE

Meet Mary Ellen Collentine. Engineer, wife, reformed rebel child.

Mary Ellen grew up in a house filled with boys. In her adolescence, she was very much a tomboy surrounded by three younger brothers. Her journey to finding her career as an engineer is a circuitous one that started with her dropping out of high school.

THE MORE YOU KNOW

When Mary Ellen dropped out of high school, it wasn't because she was failing her classes. She remarked on her academic record, "I did pretty well until I got derailed in middle school. I went through a pretty strong rebellious period. But in grade school, I was always good in my math classes." When she made the decision to drop out of high school, Mary Ellen moved out of her parents' home. The act of moving out was her form of rebellion against some of the structures in the home she grew up in. She said of her parents, "My parents are very nice people but there wasn't support for anything too radical as far as a career choice."

To finish out her high school education, Mary Ellen took summer courses to finally get her diploma. At that point, she had no idea she wanted to be an engineer. The job title was so far beyond her knowledge and experience that there was no way for her to have considered it as an option. The only thing Mary Ellen knew she wanted was to do something where she could support herself. As she put it bluntly, "In other words, I didn't want to invest in marriage as my form of economic support." At the time, that was the choice many young women made, but Mary Ellen was far from conventional in her decision-making. She knew that if she wanted financial independence, it was her responsibility to find a career path that would make that happen.

After taking night classes at the local community college with the goal being to go to a state university, Mary Ellen earned a spot at Humboldt State. "It was as far north as I could get without having to pay out-of-state tuition. I had no clue what I wanted to do. And I think I went through about ten different majors." All she knew was that she needed an education. What she would study was still up in the air! Mary Ellen tried Sociology then got really into the sciences, which led to her taking more math classes.

Eventually, she accumulated enough pre-requisite credit for different types of science majors, and she had an epiphany! Mary Ellen recalls, "I think it was while I was under nitrous oxide at the dentist's office. I had this epiphany because I suddenly realized one important point about myself—I'm very practical." She switched her major from physics to engineering to move away from the more theoretical sciences. "I thought I'd try engineering. I didn't know anybody in engineering; no one in my family had ever been an engineer. It just felt right.

My parents' vision for me was either to be a teacher or a nurse. At the time, I didn't want to get pigeon-holed into what I thought were pretty female-only careers." She eventually reconciled with her parents and they helped to pay her tuition through college. Mary Ellen worked part-time as a waitress for many years to pay all of her own living expenses while in school. Before she graduated, Mary Ellen got married and, with her husband's financial support, she finished up her degree. She didn't go the easy route. Mary Ellen followed her passion for math and science into a male-dominated industry and learned quickly she was going to have to draw on her inner strength to survive.

HAZARDS OF BEING THE ONLY WOMAN IN THE ROOM
When she looks back on earning her engineering degree, Mary Ellen termed it, "A bit of a lonely experience because there were no other women to interact with."

She was resilient and used what she learned in her formative years growing up with brothers to forge relationships with the other men in the classroom. She just powered through and didn't pause to think about the fact that she was the only woman in the classroom.

Once she graduated and went out to look for a job, Mary Ellen realized the full weight of the sexism she was up against. In one interview, she distinctly remembers the male interviewer telling her that he couldn't possibly hire her because that would take her away from her husband. "I just looked at him in disbelief. I really didn't know what to say to him other than, 'I'm okay with it and my husband is okay with it.' But I could tell from the way he was interacting with me that he had his mind made up. So I just said okay and went on to find something else."

The sexism spilled over into her first job as well. She worked for a local consulting engineering firm, and they had a large sewer job they were doing in a small town. Mary Ellen prefaced her following story with the statement, "We would never do this to an engineer joining our office." She was handed a set of plans and told to go inspect the job site. "I knew nothing about what I was doing and had to learn a tremendous amount on the job, especially about how to deal with people. I got hazed by the construction crews frequently. Mostly I chose to ignore it, but not always." She often took the high road. Her role gave her a certain amount of power over them as she was in charge of approving pay, so not every crew member was bold enough to cross her, but one load operator just wouldn't leave her alone.

At the same sewer job, a load operator on the construction crew decided to mess with Mary Ellen. She stood next to a pretty deep trench that had been dug out. As a part of her job, she was overseeing the crew laying pipe at the bottom. The load operator approached Mary Ellen from behind and bumped her in the back of her legs. She lost her balance and had to jump over the trench to steady herself. She told him she didn't appreciate that and not to do it again. Of course, he did it again, causing her to jump across the trench a second time.

Mary Ellen recounted how the situation made her feel, "It really pissed me off. When you're being harassed like that, you can't always just swallow it up. So, the next time he was standing by the trench, I went up behind him and hit him really hard in the back of the legs, making him jump across the trench. But you know, it's just things like that... I had to learn the really tough way to hide my emotions and to be able to play in that world." Mary Ellen loved being an engineer, and she wasn't going to quit just because some man tried to make her feel uncomfortable in the workplace. She belonged there just as much as any of them. Mary Ellen earned her spot.

At a different engineering firm, her colleagues put up the iconic poster of Marylin Monroe over the sewer grate in the unisex bathroom to try and make her uncomfortable. Luckily, at the time, it didn't even register to her that it might have been put there specifically for her arrival. "I didn't think anything of it at the time. I just thought this is just a part of who they are here. Well, I learned later that that had been specially put up for my arrival. The guy who hired me found out about it and went over and ripped it out. I learned about this all later—when I got there on day one, I was just happy-go-lucky that I got a job in engineering. You know, I was friendly and happy and just excited to be there."

Her ignorance of the malice behind others' actions saved her from a lot of grief. When she applied for that job and was hired on, the wife of the lead surveyor called up the big boss and lobbied him not to hire Mary Ellen. The woman's reasoning was that somehow hiring a woman jeopardized her marriage. Mary Ellen shared her boss' reaction to the comment, "He just basically told her to go away. There were a lot of little things like that. Eventually, the group got used to me and we had a good relationship." She kept her nose to the grindstone and proved she was really good at her job. It took a while to build a positive relationship with her male coworkers, but Mary Ellen never gave up.

PAVING THE WAY

Mary Ellen is passionate about changing the narrative for women in engineering. When she finally made it to a hiring position, she actively recruited and hired other female engineers. It was important to her to create a safe space for women in the industry. She noted, thankfully, that the field has evolved so much since she first started and there are many women in the field today.

To create institutional change, you have to stand up for what you believe. Mary Ellen commented, "Today people are opening up about things and being more vocal about not accepting bully behavior. Before anything is going to change, you can't allow yourself to be bullied, which was so common for women in engineering at the time. You have to be able to show people they can't steamroll you and it's a difficult thing to learn to react to those situations in a professional way." It took Mary Ellen years of enduring mistreatment and trying to find her voice before she saw any progress. Even when change is slow, you have to stick to what you know to be right.

When Mary Ellen faces a difficult task, she tackles it first through a visualization exercise. Once she can envision her success, she will take action and work to make it a reality. This trick isn't limited to Mary Ellen's professional endeavors. Several years ago, she decided she wanted to tackle Mt. Whitney—a massive feat. To make it happen, she first envisioned herself climbing to the top. After seeing in her mind where she wanted to go, Mary Ellen had a clear picture to return to for motivation when the climb got tough. Envision yourself overcoming the obstacles that lay in front of you. It is the first step in the direction of success!

Pearls of Wisdom:

- Use the adversity in your life as fuel to accomplish your goals. Your resilience is your strength! If you, like Valerie Palmer, had to cross crocodile-infested rivers to get to school every day, would you let them continue to scare you each time you walked past?
- If you are in a position of authority, as Mary Ellen was, to give other women a shot at their dream career, do it! Change the narrative.
- Visualize your success before taking action. Find your version of Mary Ellen's Mt. Whitney and then climb it!

Chapter 10

Inspiration is Anywhere and Everywhere

"Life is like a box of chocolates. You never know what you're gonna get."

—TOM HANKS AS FORREST GUMP, IN *Forrest Gump*[15]

Inspiration can come from anywhere. It takes all forms and often presents itself as a specially packaged reminder to live life to your core values.

---

15   Zemeckis, Robert, Steve Tisch, Wendy Finerman, Steve Starkey, Eric Roth, Don Burgess, Arthur Schmidt, et al. 2001. *Forrest Gump*. Hollywood, CA: Paramount Pictures

QUESTIONING AUTHORITY

Meet Gwen Sheridan. Mother, wife to a librarian/war vet, introvert, and startup executive.

She believes her life has a serendipitous thread running through it. Gwen explained, "More so than trying to iron out a ten-year plan, I have tried to choose things that open doors as opposed to close them, then I kind of crossed my fingers, shut my eyes, and jumped." I would argue there is a large thread woven throughout Gwen's life of her exercising the courage to seizing what appeared to her as a serendipitous opportunity.

THINKING ABOUT BIG PROBLEMS

In college, Gwen was a religion major. "I have never found anything more interesting in my whole life." Gwen was adamant that her senior thesis on Jewish and Christian demons and angels and post-second-temple apocalypse within Judea was the single most interesting topic of study. She was so engrossed in her thesis work that by the time she came up for air in March of her senior year, she remembered she needed a plan for post-grad. It was an afterthought for her. She had no idea where to start. "Thinking back on it, there was probably a career center at my college that could have helped me figure this out sooner, but it just never registered to check it out!" How could any job measure up to her love of studying angels and demons?

A small company growing quickly out of DC was hiring. She could still sign up for interviews, even though she was late in her job search. She chatted with a few friends of hers that joined the company a year prior who absolutely loved it. Gwen decided living in DC would be fun so she decided to close her eyes and jump, saying yes to the job at what was then known as The Advisory Board Company and today is Gartner. Once she got settled into her role, she was surprised by how much she actually liked the work she was doing. Gwen recalled, "What I didn't know was that business research and business strategy was almost—not quite, but almost—as interesting as researching in an academic setting. I couldn't believe that I got paid for essentially thinking about really complicated problems with a certain audacity that I, at age twenty-two, had something to teach insurance executives who had been doing this for thirty years."

Gwen loved her job so much that she decided to go back to business school in order to learn as much as she possibly could. "I started to make a couple of very deliberate moves to make me a more appealing candidate for business school." Most notably, at the Advisory Board Company, there was a fork in her career path. She had to choose to go the people manager route or stay in her individual contributor role. "I picked the people manager route explicitly because I thought that role specifically was going to make me a better candidate for business school. For the first time in my career, I got a lot of pushback."

BEING TOLD YOU ARE WRONG

Gwen mentioned there were several times in her career when managers told her she was making the wrong call by pursuing the paths she chose to walk down. In this first instance, two leaders in the company who were at the Managing Director and C-Level advised her not to take the role that would take her off their team. She was a top performer; they didn't want to lose her talent. "They were thinking about what was better for the business, not what was better for me. I had this moment of realization that these were two men that I liked and respected but, in that situation, they were misleading me. Or at a minimum, they didn't put my interests before the business. I thought, 'Okay, thank you for your time, but I am going to do what I want to do.'" She stuck to her guns, even taking a loss in earning potential.

Her decision to take the people manager job over the individual contributor role meant she would sacrifice

$5,000 in salary. At that point in her life, $5,000 was a lot of money. Her manager also forced her to stay in her role an extra five months to finish out a project her team had just started. Gwen thought this was ridiculous. "They made me agree to the lower pay and then they were going to make me wait an extra couple of months to start." She tried to negotiate the higher salary to make up for the ludicrous demand they were making of her and, of course, they shot her idea down.

As a result, the unfortunate situation caused an enormous rift between her and her direct boss. They eventually made up, yet she no longer trusted him to represent her interests to the company as managers should strive to do. Gwen shifted her entire mindset. "From that day forward, I had to learn to get comfortable with the idea that I had to figure this life and career path thing out on my own." She learned how to introspectively evaluate her goals against the advice she was given. Gwen courageously soldiered on in the direction she wanted to go to make her dream of attending one of the top five business schools in the country a reality.

GOOD KARMA

Spoiler alert: she got into her first-choice business school. But wait, there's more... The company paid her tuition!

Shortly after, Gwen got an offer to go work for the CEO of the company as his chief of staff. She said of the experience, "I loved my boss; he was such a good mentor, and he was so smart. It made me really want to do well for him as well as for myself and the company." She took the opportunity and jumped in with two feet from the get-go.

At this point in her life, Gwen found her "buddy," the man she knew she would marry. Unfortunately, he got deployed to Afghanistan right before she started this new job. She was grateful those two years he was overseas aligned with this job. "The one upside was it happened to overlap with those two years of being chief of staff, which in retrospect, was such good luck. I mean, if you have to have the love of your life maybe get killed, this was a good time to do it." She could be really busy and distract herself from the things she couldn't control. Gwen was adamant that as the chief of staff, she worked the hardest she ever had in her life. Her workweek consisted of eighty-five- or ninety-hour weeks and she even worked one and a half days on the weekend. At that point in her life, she could and she wanted to!

UP FOR THE CHALLENGE

After two years in her chief of staff role, Gwen was getting ready to leave. She thought deeply about what she wanted her career trajectory to look like and, at the end of the day, she wanted to be a general manager. Gwen took this goal to a trusted mentor and friend. She explained to him the logic behind her decision, and he shot back, "Well, that's never going to work out for you. No general manager ever gets to that position without having been in a sales role. You have to understand what it's like to set a goal to achieve revenue and learn how to deal with the consequences of missing that goal." He threw in at the end, "Plus, I don't think you could ever ask for money."

Gwen was so hurt by that statement that it took several days to truly process what he meant by the advice he was giving her. "I think it was so big an insult to me that I actually didn't get it at first. In the moment, I just accepted what he said but then, several days later, I had that 'wait... what?' moment." She had to get mad to accept the challenge he threw down before her. When she could think clearly on his advice, she internalized the bits and pieces that inspired her to ask for the shot at a revenue-carrying role.

In Gwen's life, she was used to being told she couldn't do something as fuel to help her accomplish her goals. She found within herself the courage to pursue her path, in whatever direction she decided to take, regardless of the noise being made by those around her. Find strength in being told no and the courage and conviction to do whatever you want to do anyway!

COACHING THE COACH

Meet Gillian Crismier. Strong businesswoman, powerful mother of two boys, loving wife, and dedicated coach.

SPORTS TEACHES LIFE SKILLS

Once upon a time, Gillian was a Girl's Select Basketball Coach. She summed up her coaching experience by dubbing it a positive one, filled with learning moments. Gillian absolutely loved the on-and-off the court coaching element, spending time to really get to know the girls on her team.

The girls motivated her to keep coming back each year! It wasn't necessarily the skills-based improvement that gave Gillian the most pride. The amount of personal growth she saw in her players was inspiring. She witnessed everything from lightbulb moments to slow and steady skill building year in and year out that gave her the distinct sense of pride that only beaming parents and other coaches will understand.

"I think sports have such a huge impact on all kids but particularly with young girls," commented Gillian. In her experience, they teach self-confidence, composure, teamwork, and inspire competitive fire. All of which are essential life skills that when learned at a young age can set girls up to learn what it feels like to succeed and be empowered by that accomplishment. "I know a lot of women will disagree with this comment, but I think a lot of boys have more natural instincts to a lot of that," Gillian said, referring to those essential life skills. As a former college athlete, Gillian understood the value of sports on a personal level. When she decided to coach, she wanted to share what she learned with other young girls. Gillian strongly believes, "Sports can bring it out in young females, you know, the competitiveness when dealing with wins, losses, sportsmanship, and everything in between."

The coping mechanisms learned through sports stretch across the personal and reach into the professional realm. A study, published in the Women in Sport and Physical Activity Journal by Human Kinetics in 2017[16], dove into how athletic participation, among other factors, can affect students' leadership skills. The authors of the study found student-athletes scored dramatically higher than

16 Torres Burtka, Allison. "Studies Show Athletes Bring Leadership Skills To The Work Place". *Globalsport Matters*, 2018.

non-athletes in overall transformational leadership. The two elements in which student-athletes excelled the most were: management of self (including attitudes toward oneself and consideration for others' well-being) and management of feelings (including motivating coworkers to elicit feelings of competence and meaning from their work).

Gillian employed those skills in many a professional situation. As an example, she mentioned, "In your office environment, you collaborate with people of different ages, backgrounds, genders, etc. and it is vital to understand how to effectively communicate and work with all of those individuals. Use those different perspectives to your advantage when critically solving a problem or working on a project. Each individual contributes something toward achieving the common goal of whatever project you are working on so knowing how to work within a team is essential." She believes the element of professional life that most closely resembles playing on a sports team is having to learn to work with different types of people—you have to communicate effectively! That communication element can make or break the success of a company's culture.

PREPARATION AND HEART SET UP THE WIN

In her initial job search, Gillian sought out a company culture that reflected who she was and who she wanted to become. She did her due diligence, looking holistically at the lifestyles of the leadership team and the core values of the people who would be her peers. "I just knew they were my people. They were former athletes, they have families, they are hard workers, and they also have work-life balance." She saw leaders within the company leaving early to be able to make their kids' sports games. As a mom who aspires to coach her own kids one day, this was a huge positive in working for the company. "I want to be able to leave at 3 PM to coach my sons, and I wanted that to not only be accepted but encouraged!"

At work, Gillian tackles her consultative sales role much the way she would a big game. "A lot goes in to close a deal," she explained, "similarly to how you would prep for a big game or a state championship or one of the other big athletic milestones I've been a part of. The level of practice and strategy that goes into preparing beforehand will make or break your outcome." She described working on a team of consultative sellers as similar to identifying the starting team in basketball. "When you're preparing, everyone in the meeting has to know their roles in order for it to be a success. So similarly to strategizing for a basketball game, you have to assign who will point guard then who will play center. Identifying those roles in advance helps tremendously to set the tone walking in. A lot of success in sales, like in sports, comes from the preparation beforehand." Gillian loves that element of her job; she gets to coach, be a team-player, and use her competitive drive to win every day she walks in the office!

Before having kids, Gillian would get in early and stay late to make sure she was prepared for her next day. Since becoming a mother, she's realized she just can't do that anymore. Gillian was surprised to find she didn't need to work the long hours to turn out the results she was looking for. Once she engaged her mom mode and learned to work hyper-efficiently, she has been more successful in her role than ever before! "Since I've had my first son, my production has actually increased. I've sold more and I work more efficiently—no longer doing those long hours. Everyone knows I have a hard stop at 4 PM when I leave the office to go relieve our nanny, and that I am unreachable between 5 PM and 8 PM until my son goes to sleep. I will log back on for a few minutes after that to answer any burning questions, but working those long hours just isn't my priority anymore." Gillian is so focused on being engaged as a mom in this season of her life that it ranks above all else for her at the moment. "I want to be a successful salesperson but I want to be an even more successful mom." The two aren't mutually exclusive in Gillian's case. She has found a way to target her energy and use her strong interpersonal skills to turn out impressive results in the office.

WORK ETHIC CHANGES THE GAME

As a coach, Gillian was able to impact young girls and empower them to be the best version of themselves. As a professional, Gillian lives that truth. She harnessed the competitive fire she exercised through sports and took her teamwork mentality into a career in sales. In her professional world, the skills of self-confidence, composure, and teamwork have helped her climb the ranks, earning highly-sought-after accolades along the way. Gillian is not alone in her success. In 2014, ESPN-W and the EY Women Athletes Business Network[17] surveyed 400 women on four continents. They found that seventy-four percent said a background in sports can help accelerate a woman's career and sixty-one percent said involvement in sports contributed to their career success.

Was playing sports a contributing factor to Gillian's success? The evidence suggests yes. Those essential life skills have helped her along this journey working toward building a life she is happy living. As the mom of two

17   espnW.com. "Study: Women + Sports = Executive Success". *ESPN.Com*, 2014.

young boys, she hopes to get involved with their future sports teams and help to nurture those same life skills through playing sports.

Approach your job—and your life—like you would your favorite sport. Teamwork makes the dream work. Let your confidence in your abilities shine!

TAKING A SABBATICAL

Meet Elaine Gibbons. "Change management" queen, mother, wife, British native, and avid traveler.

Fun fact: Elaine has created a role and job title for herself at almost every company she has worked for throughout her career. Her skill set is unique and often something that most organizations overlook, but it makes all the difference in the culture of the company.

Elaine executes large-scale change management. She was insistent that, "Although it sounds terribly dull, it really isn't. It is essential for improvement, it's essential for innovation, it's essential for building, creating, motivating at the staff level." Elaine has found herself in many situations where she is tasked to get initiatives started and build out new functions, operating models, and teams. It forced her to learn to be comfortable, flexible, and adaptable to changing environments. Little did she know that down the road, she would take her professional skills and apply them to her personal life to manage a season of uncertainty and guide herself through it to an opportunity tailor-made for her skillset.

CHANGE IN LOCATION

A new CEO brought a new strategy of cost management and productivity improvement with the intent of starting corporate operations in India. The CEO brought in a global consulting group to develop the business case. The case, although cost-effective, did not take into account very important elements of the transformation— the culture, the people, the long-term sustainability and success of such a global organization. If they didn't take care of the people being brought into the fold and work to onboard and incorporate them into the company then the company would lose out in the long run.

Elaine and her team recognized these issues and called attention to it. She explained that there needed to be someone who managed the initiative with more than an eye to just cost, who considered the transition of people, culture, and helped the company to adapt quickly to the new business model. Although that intangible element is hard to assign a dollar value to, the CEO heard her out and decided she was the right person to lead the work. Elaine spoke up and went against the grain and fought for people who in that moment didn't have a voice. Ultimately, they flourished as a result!

She was sent to Bangalore, India to live, work, and manage operations. For Elaine and her family, it was an exciting adventure. Although she would be gone for two years from friends, Elaine had an incredibly positive outlook on the chance to move to India, "The other side of sacrifice is tremendous opportunity. I do think of those two things as constantly requiring to be balanced in some way." Elaine had already spent time in India and did her first year of schooling in the country. Elaine mentioned, "I had lived in India when I was five years old. I did my first year of school in India, and so for my son to do his first year in India was a very nice reminder of how life can repeat itself." In many regards, her move to India was one of the coolest opportunities she ever had the chance to experience. It stretched both her personal and professional boundaries and was a wonderful chance to travel around Asia and experience many new cultures.

CHANGE IN PERSPECTIVE

The other side of that opportunity, as Elaine mentioned, was sacrifice. She recalled making the decision to move,

"There is tremendous sacrifice as well in an experience like that. You must have a high tolerance for ambiguity and you must be really risk tolerant. In the move, I sacrificed a lot of that consistency I had in my everyday life." She also mentioned the sacrifice of proximity to loved ones as being one of the most difficult challenges to deal with for those who are family-oriented or have close relationships.

On the point of sacrifice, Elaine noted that as an ambitious woman who loves to work, there are moments she has sacrificed over the years that have added up in a big way. She elaborated, saying, "It's common, in circles of ambitious women, to discuss the sacrifice made on sharing the small moments in your life every day with whoever you share that with—spouse, kids, dog, whatever it may be! There's that level of daily sacrifice that I think one has to be very careful about because you can look up in three years and realize that you've missed out on so many small moments that collectively you end up missing out on a lot more than you thought. I think it's very easy to overlook. I've done it myself without ever realizing it."

Elaine shared a small example of how she's worked to combat that daily level of sacrifice. In her current role, she travels a ton to far off corners of the world. In the past, she has booked flights that logistically made the most sense. Those flights often meant she would give up her Sundays with family. Those Sundays added up quickly and she missed out on some shared moments. In order to prevent that going forward, she factors family time into her travel schedule when possible to avoid missing quality time spent together as much as possible.

Another dimension of sacrifice that Elaine is really conscious of is that not all sacrifice is of equal magnitude for every woman. She has a huge amount of respect for the sacrifice of low-income families and women of color who make a much more fundamental type of sacrifice when it comes to leaving their family for work. "It is often in service to others. As working mothers, we all make the sacrifice of spending time with our kids, but for women of color or in low-income households that sacrifice often tends to be in service of others. Often benefitting women of privilege to help raise their children, and clean their houses, and do their laundry. It's something to reflect on that while it can feel hard, there is quite a different level of sacrifice for women of privilege."

CHANGE IN PURPOSE

After her time in India was up, the company she worked for offered Elaine a similar role in the UK. It didn't present the same exciting challenge as moving to India had just two years prior so Elaine made the radical decision to decline the job and leave the company in search of a role that really pushed her to do more. For a year, Elaine was on sabbatical, spending her time networking and doing some introspective work to find out what she was really passionate about.

She has a talent for change management projects and building new things, and Elaine wanted to apply that skillset at a mission-driven organization where she could make an impact on the global community. "I realized after much thoughtful networking that I wanted to work at an organization that valued a mission-driven social purpose and was a complicated global organization undergoing change but with strong strategic leadership." She was pointed in the direction of Path, a global health Nonprofit.

The CEO, Steve Davis, whom she now reports to, brought Elaine in to build out a new function in their organization, which was focused on building more strategic private sector industry partnerships. She describes her experience at Path as filled with building new things and solving really tough but interesting challenges. "We develop vaccines, diagnostics, drugs, medical devices, and health technologies for broken markets. Industry is always a critical partner and we needed to build more partnerships that were strategic and long term. We also needed to engage new sectors, like tech. So that's what we set out to do." Since then, the CEO has asked Elaine to take on a broader role in the organization and she now runs all of Path government affairs, marketing communications, and partnerships and fundraising portion for the organization, globally. Her team is dispersed around the world from Nairobi to Seattle. Elaine is never bored. She loves the amount of travel involved in her work and the impact her teams make across the globe.

Elaine used her time off to focus her skillset into an area where she could make the most impact. Be introspective about what drives you. The first step toward fulfillment is on the other side

Pearls of Wisdom:
- You can find inspiration to pursue your goals in many forms:
- Being told no can light the fire inside of you to tackle your goal head-on. As Gwen found the courage within herself to push past the no, so too can you!
- Playing a sport can teach you so many valuable lessons. Gillian applies the game-time mentality she cultivated playing sports to her sales career. The life skills she learned being a part of a team and honing

her individual talents have helped her to find success in her chosen professional.

- Making a risky decision can inspire you to take a hard look at what is important to you. Time off can often bring clarity. Elaine used her sabbatical to find a role that fulfilled her "why" at a time of transition in her life.

Chapter 11

Defiance Gets Things Done

"You may call me a dreamer but I'm not the only one..."

—"IMAGINE" BY JOHN LENNON[18]

GUCCI GOALS

Meet Jess McMahon. Boy mom, project manager, and supportive partner.

When I told Jess the story of what fueled me to write this book, her knee-jerk reaction was, "What incredible fuel to accomplish your goals!" Her outlook on life

---

18   Solt, Andrew, Sam Egan, and Yōko Ono. 1988. *Imagine:*
John Lennon. New York: Macmillan Pub. Co.

and unwavering ambition are next-level. From her own experience, she advised, "When you have big dreams, you are going to constantly run into people who don't understand your vision—especially in a creative field. The positive is that your biggest fans float to the top right away!"

By day, Jess is a project manager at a technology company. Outside of her day job, Jess is the manager of an alternative band signed with Sony Music. This side hustle didn't come into the picture until five years ago. Prior to finding this gig, Jess went through several big life events that sent her down the path she was meant to walk.

ROLE-MODELING

Having a child changed Jess' entire life. "I expected to love him. But I didn't expect to feel this overwhelming responsibility to live a big life for him. As his parent, how am I supposed to tell this little person, 'You can do anything you want,' when I'm not doing that myself?" Jess felt a responsibility to role-model what it looks like to be a big dreamer for her son. She took a hard look at her life and the people in it and revisited her personal goals.

In the end, she made the decision to leave her son's dad. When asked about her decision, Jess shared, "This comfortable life of a big house with a picket fence in the suburbs just wasn't working for me. I didn't know specifically why, but it just wasn't." Jess and her ex-partner decided to split time with their son 50/50 and have developed a very successful co-parenting relationship as a result.

A DIFFICULT DECISION WITH A BIG PAY-OFF

Her choice to leave was the catalyst for major opportunity to come knocking on her door! At the time, Jess was working for Rhapsody—the first music streaming service. In her role as Marketing Manager, she was running events and putting on music festivals. A fringe benefit of her role was meeting the band she now manages. After building a solid working relationship through Rhapsody, the band tapped Jess and asked her to be their manager. She was shocked, and says, "I was so confused at the time why they asked me to manage them. It was never something I thought of doing in my life." Jess considered all angles of the opportunity before making a decision, and in the end, she couldn't say no. "We started on this uncertain journey together. That was five years ago. Today, managing the band has become my ultimate creative passion project. Those two men have become my family and together we are trying to achieve the impossible dream of 'making it.' This creative outlet feeds my soul and has allowed me to completely express myself."

When thinking about what her life would look like with a child and career, Jess never envisioned the way it has turned out. Jess still works a corporate job Monday through Friday in addition to managing the band. She is the proud co-parent of an eight-year-old boy who is the center of her world. She found the love of her life and commutes every other weekend (when she doesn't have her son) to Calgary to see him. She is also in the process of starting her own side business in relation to managing the band. "My life seems a little bit chaotic for folks. But it's my managed chaos with everything that I love in it."

In building her life full of "managed chaos," Jess has found genuine happiness. People are drawn to her positivity. She remembers being asked quite a few times over the past couple of years if she was genuinely happy with her life. Her response is a resounding yes! "People are skeptical when I say I am really genuinely happy. When I say that, I don't mean that there aren't tough days. Of course, I still run into a**holes that make me question everything that I've chosen to do in my life. At the end of the day or even the next morning, I remind myself that everything I am doing has purpose and that other's opinions have no bearing on what I think of my life. F*ck that guy, right? It's not his life!"

GROWING PAINS

Jess believes she is the best version of herself today and is proud of her accomplishments. In growing into this "best version" of herself there were some growing pains.

Many people didn't understand her decision to leave her son's father. "I had my boss pull me aside one day to talk about it. There were friends of mine that I never ever thought would leave my life that just stopped talking to me. They kept asking me if I understood the impact of my decision." Ultimately, Jess made the decision she thought was best for her and her son. It was hard for Jess to let those people flow out of her life, yet she held firmly to her belief that she made the right choice.

When she started managing the band, she recounted the reactions of those around her. "People laughed at me when I told them initially about this new endeavor. Whether it was coworkers, friends, or even the person I was dating at the time, they all kind of brushed off the idea and didn't really think I could do it." Jess noticed something interesting associated with those who reacted negatively to her goals. Many of the people she told about her dreams weren't happy with their own lives. All Jess really wanted to find in pursuing something creative was happiness.

Those two big life events—leaving her son's father and deciding to manage a band—elicited a strong reaction from the people around her. "It eliminated a big group in my life but welcomed in a smaller group of people who were also big dreamers." By surrounding herself with a group of people who understood her vision and support her goals, Jess set herself up well for later down the road. "Now every time that I've had a hard day, or I'm unsure about something, I have this network of people that I can lean on who get it. They are incredibly positive and supportive. It is absolutely critical to have those people in your life, even if it's only a few."

RESTRUCTURING HER RELATIONSHIP WITH FAILURE

Backed by a group of supportive 'big dreamers' and refocused on pursuing her own happiness, Jess restructured her relationship with failure. She decided she would rather try managing a band, give it everything she had, and fail rather than not try at all. "I convinced myself to let this be its own experience. Any way it turned out; I would grow from it. If it doesn't work, so what! I had to let myself off the hook a bit for things rather than put so much pressure on myself." By taking the pressure off to succeed, Jess was able to get over the first hurdle in working toward her dream. Many never make it past that step because they are paralyzed by fear of failure. Jess stopped thinking about what she should be and started thinking about what she could be and that made all the difference in her outcome.

Jess is a self-described ambitious female. This classification comes with its own unique challenges. "I think being an ambitious female, we feel this intense responsibility to show that we have it together all the time. While I definitely still try to come off that way, at the same time, I kind of personally let myself say, *it's okay, Jess—if this doesn't work, this is one thing. Fine. You'll try something else.*" Making the decision to let herself off the hook for failure was incredibly scary. However, each time she tried something new and different and gave herself the freedom to fail, she got more comfortable trying new things. Once she incorporated that practice into her life, putting herself out there got less scary every time she did it and the personal growth payoff has been huge.

DEFINING SUCCESS

To focus her energy toward a positive outcome, Jess visualized what she wants her success to look like so she knows when she has arrived. It looks like Gucci socks. Jess explained, "I want to be backstage while the guys play a major stadium, and I want to have Gucci socks on. I still want to be me, in a pair of black jeans and a black t-shirt with my leather jacket. Right? But I want a pair of Gucci socks on. Socks are something people don't see. They are just for me." Her crew of big-dreamers immediately got her vision and what the socks symbolize. Others have reacted with confusion and even laughed in her face. When people tell Jess they don't know what the Gucci socks mean, her response is, "That's okay!" She explains it isn't about the Gucci brand at all. They symbolize the fact that she can buy something expensive for herself just because she can and do so without being flashy.

Find your own way to define your success. Don't worry about whether other people understand it because it is only for you. Whatever it is keep it in focus and use it to motivate yourself. You go, big dreamer!

GOING AGAINST THE STATUS QUO
Meet Chelsey White, CPA.

This former public accountant was featured in Instagram's Story Highlights rollout video. No, she wasn't crunching numbers or looking at financial statements. Chelsey White was decorating a cake. Her awesome Pink Drip Cake to be exact.

THE START OF SOMETHING DELICIOUS

Now, most people who are passionate about baking or cooking have an origin story that is based around family time in the kitchen. Chelsey breaks that mold entirely. "I literally did not bake from scratch until I moved to New York. I made a batch of cookies for my team at work and people seemed enthusiastic enough about it."

This enthusiasm from her co-workers was just enough spark to inspire her to keep experimenting in the kitchen as she worked 100+ hours a week at Ernst & Young fresh out of college. She performed financial audits, guiding clients through the extensive process. Her job became a lifestyle as it demanded her to work through the weekend. When talking about her workload, Chelsey candidly shared, "There is nothing worse than being an auditor at a public accounting firm."

To unwind after a long hard day, Chelsey took up baking. A coworker's birthday was coming up and a lightbulb went off in her head. Why not make her a cake! "I really went to town making this cake. It was hideous but still delicious." The birthday honoree was flattered and her coworkers enjoyed the delicious treat. Soon, she was making cakes by request for birthday celebrations for other teams within the company. Even when she got home at 10 PM and had to have a cake ready the next day for a colleague, Chelsey would stay up until 2 AM just to get it done.

CHOOSING TO CHANGE YOUR LIFE

Finance is extremely demanding of your time. When she made the switch from EY to L'Oréal, her schedule changed—freeing up her weekends. "I was working until nine at night, but I wasn't working weekends. That was huge because when you're working weekends and you're working late, life becomes impossible. You just aren't sleeping. One thing has to give."

The thing that Chelsey chose to sacrifice was her job at EY. She needed to sleep and she also had dreams of formalizing her cake-making hobby into a business. When she made the switch to L'Oréal, with her weekends finally free, Chelsey filed for her business license making Chelsweets officially official. "I was baking stuff for quite a while. So one day, I made myself go get a business license. Before then, I was making cakes for people and selling some of them. However, this formality just made it more of a real thing to me and encouraged me to sell more." On that very same day, Chelsey ordered cake boxes and stamps and business cards—all branded and ready to be put to use!

Chelsweets took off through word of mouth—no paid media required. Chesley kept expanding her base of business one satisfied cake client at a time. Friends of hers would request cakes, then when they saw how beautifully decorated they were and tasted the delicious result, those friends would tell their friends. Building her customer base was akin to a grassroots movement—those who were passionate about her cakes were, in turn, vocal about their adoration of her work. Chelsey describes the organic growth Chelsweets experienced as "spiraling out of control." She was, of course, sharing her creations on Instagram from time to time, but that was before the concept of 'influencers' emerged. It was not trendy—yet! These orders were coming from people she knew who told their friends and then friends of those friends. She received so many orders, it was almost overwhelming what she could accomplish while still working full time.

DIVING HEADFIRST INTO BEING AN ENTREPRENEUR
Chelsey took Chelsweets on full time in January of 2019. After four years of baking while working in the finance

world, it was time for a change. This decision to continue to work while making her entrepreneurial start she attributes to her "cautious" personality. However, her path is emblematic of a greater trend in entrepreneurial success.

A fifteen-year study[19] was conducted by researching and tracking more than 5,000 entrepreneurs in the United States as they established their own ventures. These entrepreneurs were anywhere from twenty to sixty years old and breaking into many different businesses. The goal of this study was to determine whether entrepreneurs were more or less successful in their ventures when they decided to keep or quit their day jobs. The conclusion? Entrepreneurs were thirty-three percent less likely to fail in their new business ventures if they remained at their day job for at least a period of three years. The research suggests Chelsey made the right move!

This cautious approach to launching her business is in line with other extremely successful entrepreneurs who also happened to be in the category of "risk-avoiders." A *Thrive* article[20] names a few. The most notable of which

---

19 Raffiee, Joseph and Jie Feng. "Should I Quit My Day Job?: A Hybrid Path To Entrepreneurship | Academy of Management Journal". *Journals.Aom.Org*, 2013.

20 Curtin, Melanie. "A 15-Year Study Of 5,000 Entrepreneurs Finally Answers The Question: Is It Better To Quit Your Day Job Or Keep It?". *Thriveglobal.Com*, 2018.

were Phil Knight of Nike, who stayed at his day job for five years before launching the successful sneaker brand, and Sarah Blakely, who developed the idea for her company Spanx over many years and continued to sell fax machines before committing to Spanx full time (her company is now estimated to be worth $1 billion).

These risk-averse people essentially buy themselves time. Those who jump right in do not have the luxury of slowing down to get it right. Melanie Curtain, author of the article "A 15-Year Study of 5,000 Entrepreneurs Finally Answers the Question: Is It Better to Quit Your Day Job or Keep It?"[21] insists that, "When you wait and have stability and security while you're building your side business, it gives you more time in general. You have more time to evaluate the marketplace, test things out and then rework them. You're not so desperate for something to work that you're misreading information." Chelsey operated this way.

BECOMING AN INFLUENCER

If you scroll back on her YouTube channel to the first video she ever posted decorating a cake, you will

---

21 Curtin, Melanie. "A 15-Year Study Of 5,000 Entrepreneurs Finally Answers The Question: Is It Better To Quit Your Day Job Or Keep It?". *Thriveglobal.Com*, 2018.

watch her create a wonderfully creative Hi-Chew candy-themed cake. This design was a request from a friend who worked at an advertising agency whose client was Hi-Chew. I was blown away by the idea of working with well-known brands. Chelsey explained to me that, "When companies lack funds in their advertising budget, they send you unlimited product. It was great, but after a while, there is only so much candy that I can and should eat." This cake produced for Hi-Chew was one of her first experiences doing an unpaid partnership. Chelsey recalled, "It was exciting for me at the time because it was all so new."

HOW TO BECOME AN INFLUENCER

Being an influencer is a hot trend that everyone wants to hop on. Chelsey's take is that forcing the situation won't take you to the top. She had three powerful pieces of advice for anyone trying to break into the influencer space:

1. Going into it with the mindset "I want to be an influencer" is the wrong approach.

Chelsey is a strong advocate of authentically sharing content she is passionate about. It's hard to find that thing that sparks joy in you so she feels extremely lucky to be able to make a career out of sharing her cakes with the world. If you are attempting to be an influencer because you see an unoccupied niche and you aren't unbelievably passionate about it, you will fail. Chelsey is convinced that because she led with her passion and put in the hard work, it shows in the quality of her content and the growth of her business.

2. You're going to have to work really really really hard.

It takes an incredible work ethic and unwavering determination because everyone second guesses themselves now and then. It definitely takes a certain strength of character to continue in the face of resistance. There are only twenty-four hours in a day and when you are the sole person managing all social media channels, content production and distribution, and seeking out new business, your time can get away from you pretty quickly.

If you're doing your job as an influencer, then the posted content feels natural and effortless to your followers. In all actuality, Chelsey has so much on her plate that it can be difficult to maintain the brand she's built. "The amount of work that goes into truly posting frequent content every day that is high quality, creative, and innovative takes so much work. This is especially the case if you're trying to do it across different platforms like YouTube, Instagram, Facebook, and a blog if you have one. It all adds up so quickly in terms of time."

3. Get a thick skin now

Social media is such a public forum. Everyone has an opinion. It is necessary to develop a thick skin. Chelsey recalls a specific comment someone posted on one of her videos hating the plastic piping bags she uses to ice her cakes. The commenter said that Chelsey was doing terrible things to the environment and that she should be using reusable piping bags. They continued nailing her, saying she has a social responsibility to use reusable products because she had so many followers that she should be setting a better example. She scoffed at the incredibly specific comment saying, "I'm sorry! Sometimes you have to use a plastic piping bag. There are reusable ones but they suck to wash, and they get gross. As an influencer though, people are constantly judging you. It is hard."

The key is not to dwell on the haters and to develop coping mechanisms that can pull you out of the rut every woman finds herself in occasionally. When Chelsey is not in the mood to deal with social media or is just mentally blocked, her best trick to getting back on track is to do something physically active. It clears her head and boosts her mood. When she is stuck but has to be productive in her business, she often turns to baking for a few hours—prepping layers for cakes to be made on the weekend—as a form of therapeutic activity to right her mind. Often, by stepping away from whatever really was frustrating her and then returning to it later with a rejuvenated mindset allows her to deal with whatever was bothering her in the first place in a more productive manner.

ALWAYS BE LEARNING

Innovation is the name of the game. It is impossible to be at the forefront of the next best thing unless you are constantly immersing yourself in new technologies, techniques, and analyzing past work to create better content in the future.

Always be open to new things and try to always be improving. "I think that's kind of something my parents drilled into me. But you know, it's true. You should always be pushing yourself to improve on the things you can control. There are always new cameras coming out and new filming styles people are using. The world is constantly changing and new platforms keep popping up so it's great to be constantly pushing yourself to do your best." Be a Learn-It-All, not a Know-It-All. When you humbly evaluate your progress and see room for improvement, you can only get better. Chelsey pays close attention to the details in her videos as she edits. Whether it's the placement of the cake in the shot or the way she positions her hands as she's icing the cake, Chelsey notes the ways to incrementally improve her content to ultimately create a better experience for her loyal following and attract new followers and opportunities.

CONNECT WITH OTHERS

Although she is a one-woman show, Chelsey has built a community of influencer friends in NYC. She has met now real-life friends on Instagram who are also influencers. "A lot of the people that I'm friends with don't really do exactly what I do. Some are literally just amazing sugar cookie decorators. They're amazing at it; that is what they do. It's not what I do and sometimes they have an entirely different business model, yet they are doing great at their thing. We are on different paths even though it seems like they're both in the cake decorating sphere. In reality, it's really doing two different things. I also have food influencer friends who just like to go to restaurants all the time. I get to be their plus one to things and, in return, I give them left-over cake. It's mutually beneficial and just really fun."

Chelsey has run into people who are pushy and competitive as influencers but she's chosen not to associate with those people. According to her, when someone stakes their livelihood on influencing it changes the experience. The important thing to note is that you get to pick your tribe! Chelsey chose to keep the positive people around who share tips and tricks on camera skills instead of those who steal each other's ideas.

It is never too late to share your passion with the world. Sometimes it resonates with other people and organically grows into a beautiful professional venture that you wake up excited about every day. For Chelsey, the choice was easy. She would rather bake and ice creative cakes than stare at Excel for twelve hours a day, hating her life.

Go follow her to find some inspiration @chelsweets !

DEFIANCE IN THE FACE OF INJUSTICE

Meet Kelsey Woods, the Non-Profit Goddess.

Kelsey has the unique capacity to get people so fired up about a social cause that they feel compelled to back it any way they can! She turned a passion for social change coupled with incredible business acumen into a career that makes a tangible impact in her community. Today

Kelsey is the Senior Development Director at Friends of the Children in the Seattle area. She furthers the Friends of the Children mission by partnering with Foundations and Philanthropists to provide youth facing the toughest challenges with professional, salaried mentors throughout their primary and secondary education. When she's not working to improve her community's access to educational support, Kelsey is the mother of an adorable little girl and a partner to her husband. It is for those future generations that Kelsey passionately works to make the world a better place than she found it.

She has seen the negative aspects of income inequality and institutional racism that impact a child's development. They often manifest in the home and spread into activities at school, effecting behavior in the classroom. Friends of the Children has found that when a young child is exposed to environmental stressors, it affects their goals, values, and personal expectations. As a result, children experiencing those side effects have a dramatically reduced chance of finding personal success.

THE COST OF BEING MISSION DRIVEN

Before Kelsey joined Friends of the Children, she had her eyes on the non-profit for ten years before she actually joined the team. "I am probably the only person who will tell you this, but I took a pay-cut to get my dream job." The job came up, and she networked her way through the employee currently holding the position. Kelsey discovered the organization's needs and the role's unique challenges. Her secret weapon was the understanding of the organization and the position allowing her not only to land the job but also to hit the ground running.

"The afternoons are the best time to be in the office; kids are running around all over the office after school." Kelsey described the life that fills the office in these golden hours at work, "There is lots of laughter and conversation." One little girl, in particular, has made a habit of coming into her office. "She has come in, sat down, and made herself at home many times. I've truly come to care for her through our shared afternoons." Kelsey's bond with this young girl in the Friends of the Children program is not that of a mentor but that of a friend and confidant. Kelsey's own daughter is too young, at one-and-a-half-years-old, to have the conversations that Kelsey shares with the girl who has made a home in her office.

SMALL GESTURES ARE MOTIVATING

Mother-daughter bonding takes place in the form of swim lessons for Kelsey and her little girl. One Saturday at a community center deep in the Rainier Valley, Kelsey and her daughter spent the morning playing in the pool during a swim lesson. As they left the community center and entered the parking lot, Kelsey noticed a man standing outside of a car. He was violently angry. Not physical in his expression of that anger, yet his words were tipped in steel, hoping to cut through the glass of the car window and nick the woman behind the wheel.

Kelsey felt helpless. Her daughter sat on her hip blissfully unaware of the scene unfolding in front of them. Kelsey couldn't intervene, not when she had her daughter with her. She watched intently to see if the situation escalated further. As she focused on the car, Kelsey noticed a small hand in the back seat waving to her. It was attached to the little girl who found solace in her office. She smiled and waved enthusiastically from behind the car window at Kelsey. The scene unfolding around the young girl didn't even seem to register.

RECOMMITTING IN A BIG WAY

Upset by the aggressive confrontation she witnessed and the unfazed reaction of the little girl, Kelsey returned to work on Monday even more committed to the mission of Friends of the Children. Unfortunately, the organization's reach can only stretch so far due to capacity constraints. Kelsey wants to create real, equitable access to high-quality education for children in underserved and underrepresented communities. She is adamant that change will not happen until many voices rise up and demand it.

On her mission to create equitable education-based empowerment for all children, Kelsey plans to get involved with the public school system either through the school board or by running for public office. Kelsey wants to drive change from the ground up and allow children from underserved communities to have all the opportunities necessary to achieve their true potential.

Pearls of Wisdom:
- Find your 'why' and speak your goals out loud. Jess is motivated by showing her son he can accomplish any dream he dares to speak into the world. Those Gucci socks symbolize the success she strives for every day!
- When you are passionate about a hobby, don't settle for the day job you hate. It may be scary to sail into uncharted waters, but when you do it thoughtfully—like Chelsey—the outcome is sweet!
- Backing a cause with your whole heart will push you to realize big dreams. Pursue them fiercely! In Kelsey's case, she is so passionate about her mission for equitable education that she wants to run for

public office in order to make a bigger impact. Where will your mission-driven dreams take you?

Chapter 12

Be Your Own
Best Friend

Who would you rather hang out with, your best friend or your worst enemy?

For me, the decision is easy. Best friend every time without hesitation. I did my own little research poll and out of the twenty women I asked, all of them responded that they would rather hang out with their best friend every day. DUH! Why is it then that most people, especially women, have this propensity for negative self-talk?

Mind + Body, Not Mind Over Matter

Meet Mollie Suits. Mother, physical therapist, and positive self-talk advocate!

For the last thirty years, she has witnessed people internally fight this mental battle of telling themselves they can't do it, whether it be a physical exercise during their physical therapy session or more broadly in their daily life. "I just always have been fascinated with how the mind controls the body. I was first exposed to this in my job and then studied it in any way that I possibly could for years and years. This was before podcasts were around so I learned by reading and attending seminars and talking to anyone who was willing to teach me. I love showing people, you can do more, you can be more! You just need someone to stand beside you and clap while you're doing it."

As a physical therapist, Mollie is passionate about unlocking her clients' potential. "I just love showing people they can do more than they think they can." Her passion for overcoming personal roadblocks stems from the adversity she has faced in her own life. "I think it's actually adversity in my life that has made me who I am. It made me kind of show myself I could make it through. I had to tell myself, 'You can do anything you want. You can't let negative things stop you. You're still the same person who you have always been.'" For many people who have experienced trauma or loss, it is hard to push past their negative experiences and not let those elements of life define who they are.

Mollie is an advocate for understanding and processing your experience and then moving forward to prove to yourself you can move on and "be more" than what has happened to you. Everything can be made an insurmountable mountain unless you choose to climb. Mollie is a strong believer in taking that first step and having a cheerleader remind you that you can make it out of the woods and to the top of the mountain.

USING POSITIVE THINKING

By managing her own personal adversity and helping her physical therapy clients triumph over their own struggles, Mollie learned the importance of a positive mindset. She became passionate about showing people how their thoughts and beliefs create their happiness and success. After years of casually grabbing coffee or drinks with people who sought her out to help reframe their thinking, Mollie decided to turn her knowledge and experience into a coaching business, Living Room Learning LLC.

Whether she is teaching in the living room or the board room, her message is the same—your thoughts and beliefs create your success. In group settings, clients of Mollie's become more aware of how they get in their own way and limit their goals and dreams. The tools and techniques that her clients learn are tangible and can be put into practice immediately.

As she took on this side-hustle, there were many nay-say-ers who didn't believe she had the background or ability to make this venture a success. Their voices rose loudly above the rest saying things like: "How could you do that? You are a physical therapist! You can't! Why would you do that?" She had another business before Living Room Learning that was a product-based business. She did that for nine years, and when she started, many people said similar negative comments, "What are you doing? Are you insane?" Mollie learned that she just had to keep going. "You have to realize that the way people react to you—that's the best that they know. Believe in yourself, no matter what people around you are saying." People can only process through their own lens and experience. Their limited mindset should not be able to hinder your growth potential.

Today, Mollie has worked with companies like Nike and is continuing to grow her brand. In her first year, Mollie hit her yearly goal within the first three months. The sky is the limit for Mollie because that is what she tells herself!

WHO RUNS THE WORLD?

One of Mollie's passions is empowering women. She teaches them how to take a deeper look at their thoughts and beliefs and scrutinize how they are holding themselves back. When she started breaking into the corporate setting, she had to rebrand her material in a more gender-neutral way to apply to all people, yet her passion truly lies in helping women. "I just love empowering women and inspiring them to just want and be more. Women often play it so safe. I love it when they push beyond what they think is possible. And it's even more exciting when they actually surpass where they hoped to be!"

FAILURE IS GROWTH IN DISGUISE.
YOU ARE NOT YOUR FAILURES!

It is time to rebrand how you think about your failures. In Mollie's group workshops, she helps people identify their relationship with failure. In her experience, most people internalize failure as a personal character flaw. "Some people, when they fail at something, they then believe they are a failure. When in reality, they failed at a task but that does not change or define who they are as a person." Mollie prefers not to see herself as a failure. She has failed—absolutely—yet she doesn't see failing as a reflection of her worth as an individual. If she doesn't knock whatever she is trying to do out of the park, fine. She analyzes the situation from all angles to determine what she can do better next time to prevent a similar result.

When you are dedicated to your own personal development, you can learn to cultivate a positive mindset. Even small changes in the way you think can have a profound effect on whether you reach your full potential and succeed at achieving your goals. Mollie teaches people how to look at their beliefs and uncover the underlying drivers behind their achievements and failures through the lens of three questions: *What went right? What went wrong? What can I do better next time?* In the wake of failure, Mollie coaches clients to learn from their mistakes by encouraging them to take a deep breath and sit down with a trusted friend or colleague to evaluate their performance based on those three questions.

The classic reaction to failure we all experience might be something akin to this:

Wow, I'm ashamed, I did not do well on that project. I just made a total fool of myself in front of everybody. I'm so embarrassed.

Mollie coaches clients to adopt a positive mindset by encouraging them to take a deep breath and sit down with themselves or someone else to evaluate their performance.

What went right? I had a relevant topic for the audience. What did I do wrong? Oh, God, I didn't have my presentation memorized and I paused too much. What can I do better for next time? I need to practice speaking in front of people.

They come up with a list of ways to improve so that they do not make the same mistakes next time. These positive-mindset individuals then go learn what they need to do in order to execute on that improvement.

Someone with a fixed mindset and poor self-esteem will handle the situation like this:

What went right? Nothing! I suck! What went wrong? Everything, I will never speak in public again! Wow, I am so ashamed. I just made a total fool out of myself in front of everyone. I am so embarrassed. I'm a loser. I've always known I'm a loser. I give up! What can I do better next time? There won't be a next time! I will never, ever speak in front of people again.

This negative thought pattern gets in the way of personal success. "You are the same person you were before you failed. You either did the best you could with the knowledge you had, or you just performed poorly in that particular moment. The experience doesn't make you a failure but your thoughts sure can." The most important aspect of failure is riding the learning curve. Analyze the situation and come up with a plan to create a better outcome next time. If you quit before you try again, you won't learn anything. By giving up and not putting yourself in situations that are challenging in healthy ways, you can end up stunting your own personal growth.

IF YOU'RE NOT FAILING, YOU'RE NOT TRYING

My family and I are huge skiers. When my mom taught my sister and I to ski, she had a mantra that she would repeat every single time we fell down: *If you're not falling, you're not trying.* Each time you level up in something, you will fall down because you are learning to do something you have never done before. Failing is a part of learning! Trying something new is hard for everyone. You will stumble because it is a path you have never walked before. The trick is to get back up and try again.

For Mollie, seeing the lightbulb go off in her clients' heads is the most rewarding experience. "Once you show people how their thoughts are influencing how they are interpreting their experiences, everything changes." She is proud to develop her clients' ability to recognize and stop negative thoughts right when they pop up. This skill set has given her clients the power to be and do more. So many clients have come back to Mollie and shared their personal successes. All of which were made possible by their newfound ability to rebrand their personal relationship with failure.

THE MEAN GIRL VOICE

When she does collaborative workshops for women, Mollie has a specific name for that negative voice in your mind—the "Mean Girl" voice. According to Mollie, the "Mean Girl" voice is that little voice that pops up in your head just to talk trash. It tells you that you aren't enough, you can't accomplish your goals, that your dreams are ridiculous. That voice says to quit before you begin, to play it safe when things get challenging. After you've completed a difficult task and performed poorly, this "Mean Girl" voice in your head tells you, "I told you so!"

Does this sound like anything you've ever said to yourself? Be honest. I know I have found myself spiraling down this thought pattern once or twice in my lifetime. I call it ruminating. Where you essentially marinate in your own toxic thoughts about yourself. It is not something that frequently happens to me. Generally, I am much more of the positive, self-cheerleader. My mom has told stories of me when I was little looking into the mirror at myself before a soccer game or a big test telling myself, "Drew, you got this! You can do it!".

BEST FRIEND VOICE

Positive self-talk is scientifically proven to boost self-esteem. Mollie equates positive self-talk to having your best friend right there by your side. "You can be a whole lot more effective when you are in there cheering yourself on than when you are tearing yourself down. You have the power to take control of your thoughts and not let them control you. You have the ability to choose thoughts that are encouraging and empowering, that will help you achieve your goals and dreams." By helping women to reframe their thinking and to listen to their "Best Friend" instead of the "Mean Girl" voice, Mollie is teaching women to get out of their own way. She is helping people take the first step toward reaching their full potential.

With this supportive approach she describes, Mollie hopes to teach young women the importance of a positive mindset "I work with all ages of women and I'm particularly passionate about the twenty-somethings. I think you can just help them skip a bunch of the misery if they learn these lessons young." By reframing individual thinking, Mollie hopes she can enable young women to have the tools to unlock their own success.

TALKING TO YOURSELF MAKES YOU BETTER

With a positive mindset, anything is possible. Mollie has certainly proven that one hundred times over. If you find yourself dragging yourself down, just remember to listen to your Best Friend instead of the Mean Girl in your head!

SELF-CARE

Reader, this is my favorite topic in this book. Just know that as I wrote this section, I was grinning from ear to ear with a face mask on. I chose to put an acne-blasting face mask because I—the gal who never breaks out—am wearing my stress in the form of acne on my chin. Then I started to stress about the stress acne and as a result, was trapped in a whirlpool dragging me straight down. This small act of putting on a face mask to fight one of the stressors in my life at this moment is one very minor example how to practice self-care.

YOU CAN'T POUR FROM AN EMPTY CUP

Rachel Hollis, New York Times Best-Selling Author and Media Mogul, has a similar stance to Mollie Suits on the relationship between the mind and the body. Teamwork makes the dream work and the mind and body are on the same side of the court. They function at peak performance when working in tandem. Rachel takes it one step further, calling out in Chapter 3 of her book *Girl, Wash Your Face*[22] that to force an individual to check in with themselves, the body produces "a physical reaction to an emotional problem." My body is throwing acne on my chin as the physical manifestation of a flashing warning sign. "Drew, you are too stressed. Stop treating yourself like this!"

In Rachel Hollis' case, she experienced facial paralysis. To read more on the specifics, go check out her book! It seriously changed the way I think about my life and how I take care of myself. The moral of her facial paralysis story is that—after visiting many traditional and non-traditional medical professionals—she learned it is necessary to make space for yourself to be still and relax. Firing on all cylinders and pushing yourself past your breaking point is detrimental to your physical and emotional wellbeing. By taking the time to be present

---

22   Hollis, Rachel. *Girl, Wash Your Face*. Nelson Books, 2018.

and check-in with yourself, you refill your metaphorical cup so that you can continue to help and support those around you. There are many different ways to practice self-care. I want to highlight three that can be adopted by you, Reader, immediately: meditation, exercise, and travel.

CALM YOUR MIND

Meet Caroline Reis.

This gal is a Make-A-Wish Donor Relations Specialist, doula helping women have positive labor experiences, artist, and volunteer. Caroline has many interests and often heaps a lot of different things on her plate. She often finds herself needing to take a step back and return to the present and be in the moment to show up as her best self for her donors and clients. She does this by practicing mindfulness and meditation.

Caroline painted a picture for me. "Have you ever driven through a stoplight and wondered if it was red or green? You get past it on the other side and you really don't know whether or not you just ran a red light. In that moment you were so focused on the destination you forgot to be present." Running a red light can be costly! It is important to refocus on what is in front of you and find joy in that moment.

For Caroline, her meditative practice comes in many forms on any given day. During the week, she puts in her headphones on her walk to and from the ferry as she commutes to work. "I love music, for me it is really healing." She uses that time to focus her energy on the music and get lost in it. She loves being outside and focuses on the feeling of being in fresh air. There are so many ways to tap into the present moment and dramatically increase your awareness of what is going on in the world around you.

Today, Caroline doesn't measure her happiness by how much is on her plate. She focuses on the small joys like listening to music as she walks to the ferry so that she can show up as her best self for the people around her!

MOVE YOUR BODY
Allow me to reintroduce to you Kelsey Woods, the nonprofit goddess mentioned in Chapter 11.

There are so many amazing stories Kelsey told me regarding the impact she has been able to make on her local community through her work at Friends of the

Children. Go check out her story "Defiance in the Face of Injustice" to learn what inspires her!

In a previous role at a huge national charity, Kelsey found herself weighed down by stress. She sought out an executive coach to determine what she needed to do to work through it. "I found myself feeling incredibly stressed out. And because of that, I was not the kind of leader to support my team that I wanted to be. I just couldn't be present with them." She worked backward to flush out her stressors.

What didn't she like about her job? The two hours a day she spent in traffic trapped in her car commuting. It was taking her away from her husband and daughter as well as cutting into her workday. Ultimately, Kelsey decided to make a job change to eliminate this high stressor. She took a pay cut to join an organization that makes her heart swell with gratitude and that is conveniently located ten minutes from her house.

On an ongoing basis, Kelsey's exercise habit helps her to manage other stressors as they arise. "It's yoga, it's my workout app in my living room, or it's going for a run. Whichever it may be, one of those things has to happen for me to feel balanced to be able to show up as my best self to work and for my family every day."

To make sure she is able to move her body throughout the day, Kelsey has to set expectations and schedule in advance. Sometimes, it looks like waking up early. Other times, it might require Kelsey to set an alarm for when to leave work to get to her yoga class on time. Then when you add kids into the mix, it all changes. "It gets way harder when you have a baby. You have to make it even more obvious to yourself and the people around you that it's a priority. I have started to put my classes in my calendar before the week starts. Otherwise, it doesn't happen."

Prioritize yourself so that you can show up as your best self when it counts. Move your body!

CHANGE YOUR SURROUNDINGS

Meet Haley Katsman.

I do not know how she hasn't made it on the Forbes 30 under 30 list yet. Haley earned a seat at the table by being naturally curious and not afraid to break things in order to build something better. Today, Haley is the VP of three divisions of the high-growth startup Highspot. When she came on board as employee number fourteen, Haley took a huge chance joining this young company but was up for the challenge. When she's not working, Haley has a passion for travel. Now that Highspot has gone international, she takes full advantage of the opportunity to mix business with pleasure!

In the beginning of her career at Highspot, 2015 was a big year for Haley. Just as she hired her first ten people, a once-in-a-lifetime travel opportunity came up to visit Africa! Her parents happened to be celebrating their thirtieth wedding anniversary and, after much persuasion, they caved and decided to bring Haley and her sister along for the adventure.

Don't be afraid to mark "Out of Office" on your calendar.

Haley was worried, with so many new people starting right as she was about to take off on a two-week trip, that upper management would veto her travel plans. She contemplated whether it was a good business decision to take time off during this busy season in her career. Thankfully, her father dropped a truth bomb on her before she could make the decision to stay. He told Haley, "If you take two weeks off and everything falls apart, then there are bigger problems at work. The company should be able to survive."

Even with this fresh perspective, Haley was still nervous to tell the CEO she would be taking two weeks off. She recounted the feeling of going into his office. "I remember walking in there and blurting out, 'I'm kind of going to Africa.' Without even skipping a beat, his response was, 'Where are you going in Africa?' He was nowhere near as concerned as I was about my taking time off. He even made suggestions of where to go and what to see from his own travel experience. It was a huge relief to have him tell me to just go and have fun."

The beautiful thing about traveling is that it offers you new perspective. On the trip, Haley went from learning about "survival mode" to basking in the beautiful savannah scenery. Haley raves about the amazing experience she had traveling through Africa. A huge element of that experience was the introspective work she did along the way. It showed her that when she is able to check out completely, it allows her to gain new perspective and simultaneously learn a lot about herself. As Haley reflected on her trip, she shared, "I truly think it ended up helping me be a better leader and person when I went back to work!"

By changing her surroundings and having limited access to Wi-Fi, Haley was gifted the chance to completely check out. In return, she came back to work totally refreshed and loaded with new ideas. "My innovative side really kicks in when I check out." By exercising her passion for travel, Haley was able to recharge and return to her life ready to conquer any challenges thrown her way!

Pearls of Wisdom:

- Listen to your "Best Friend," not that "Mean Girl" who is trying to dull your sparkle.
- Retrain your brain to react constructively to failure. Unlock a growth mindset and you will achieve MORE!
- Self-care. Practice it. Find out what you need to do to check in with yourself emotionally and physically. Go to Africa if that is what it takes!

Conclusion

'Having It All' In Context

This book started out as the ultimate clap back to a man who told me to Dream Smaller. But that experience was just the spark that lit the match on this project. Since then, I have interviewed more than fifty inspiring women from across the country and all different walks of life to see how they've managed to design their lives in a way that make space for their dreams. In reading this book, you've just spent time with thirty of those women, hearing about a small slice of their lives and hopefully learning from the little pearls of wisdom their experiences have to offer.

ACCEPT THE SHIFT IN SEASONS

We explored the concept of there being seasons to life and that there is no right order in which to live out those seasons. Jean Thompson offered up a new way to look at designing your life by approaching it like a balanced diet. It is unnecessary to eat every meal with perfect nutritional balance. In much the same way, you can prioritize different elements of your life in different seasons. The biggest takeaway here is that it is okay to readjust the way you prioritize the elements in your life based on what is important to you in that new season! As long as you are sticking to your values and using them as your guidepost on where to take action in your life, then you are on the right path to 'Have It All' in the context of your own life.

INVEST IN YOUR COMMUNITY

There is absolutely strength in numbers. By thoughtfully surrounding yourself with mentors, friends, partners, and family, you create a community that will build you up and support you when you need it most. We dove into the concept of community and how it plays into personal and professional success and happiness. Christine Baerwaldt showcased how to grow your community through tapping into your own vulnerability. We explored the basis of equal partnership and the many forms that may take as it is different in every relationship. In JoAnne

Kennedy's case, it comes in the form of a contract and a quarterly business review! By investing your time and energy into building a strong community, you can lean on them when life throws you curveballs. Mychele Riddick committed to building deep connections with her colleagues and when her husband got sick, those peers stepped up to help her family navigate this new season of their lives. Whether the challenges you face are tragic and life changing or smaller and more day to day, a well-curated community will lift you up to be the best version of yourself. As you enter new seasons of your life, you may find that some relationships no longer align with your trajectory. At that point, it is important to return to your values, be introspective about those relationships, and thoughtfully recycle those relationships on an as-needed basis! It is better for you and the other party to make space for those who most align with your values and purpose.

PRIORITIZE YOUR PASSIONS

Inspiration can be found anywhere and often hides in the most unsuspecting of places! Valerie Palmer and Mary Ellen Collentine used their backgrounds to fuel their vision of the future and are highlighted as examples of taking risks that ultimately inspire change. They found inspiration from their circumstances and chose to actively follow their dreams in bold new ways. Find your source of inspiration, whether it be an internal or external source and use it as motivation to push defiantly in the direction of your dreams! Do not forget to take care of yourself along the way. Be your own "Best Friend" by practicing positive self-talk. You'll be amazed by the difference changing your internal dialogue can have on the way you interact with the world. It is a superpower that will help you create your own happiness and actualize your goals. Incorporate some form of self-care into your daily routine. It can be anything from moving your body to quieting your mind. Play around with different forms of self-care until you find what helps you to be the best version of yourself so you can go out and pursue your big dreams!

MY HOPE FOR YOU

It is my dearest wish that whatever season of your life you find yourself in while reading this book that you feel like you gained a new perspective and can implement even one of the pearls of wisdom into your own life as you see fit. I want to personally thank you for picking up this book and taking the time to read through these stories. If there is someone you know who needs some tangible guidance on designing her life to make space for big dreams, please share this book with that person.

I encourage you to take a thoughtful look at the women around you and empathize with their experiences. Their situation might look different from your own but that does not mean that they don't Have It All in their own right.

I hope you dare to dream big and intentionally design your life to help make those dreams a reality. And if you EVER are told to Dream Smaller and advised to live a watered-down version of the life you want, please smack this book down right in front of that person's face. These pages tell the stories of thirty women who prove that person doesn't know what they are talking about!

This is just the beginning! I want to hear from you. If you apply any pearls of wisdom to your life and you see real change in making your dreams a reality, please share your wins with me! If you know of any women who 'Have It All' in the context of their own lives, please introduce them to me via email dreamsmaller2019@gmail.com. I would love to continue to learn!

Join the conversation! If you are a big dreamer or looking to connect with other inspiring women and men striving to design their lives to 'Have It All' in their own way, then head on over to Facebook and join the Dream Smaller with Drew group.

https://www.facebook.com/groups/dreamsmaller/

I challenge you to write a dream down on this page and chase it with your whole heart. The best is yet to come!

Works Referenced

Chapter 1

Graham, Daniel W., "Heraclitus", *The Stanford Encyclopedia of Philosophy* (Fall 2019 Edition), Edward N. Zalta (ed.), URL <https://plato.stanford.edu/archives/fall2019/entries/heraclitus/>. (August 3, 2019)

Hollis, Rachel. *Girl, Wash Your Face.* Nelson Books, 2018.

Chapter 2

Paré, Elizabeth and Heather Dillway. ""Staying at Home" versus "Working": A Call for Broader Conceptualizations of Parenthood and Paid Work." *Michigan Family Review,* no. 10(2005): 66-87. url: https://quod.lib.umich.edu/cgi/p/

pod/dod-idx/staying-at-home-versus-working-a-call-for-broader.pdf?c=mfr;idno=4919087.0010.105;format=pdf.

Chapter 3

Khazan, Olga. "The Rise Of Older Mothers". *The Atlantic*, 2018. https://www.theatlantic.com/health/archive/2018/05/the-rise-of-older-mothers/560555/.

"Yoga Statistics: Staggering Growth Shows Ever-Increasing Popularity". *The Good Body*, 2018. https://www.thegoodbody.com/yoga-statistics/.

Chapter 4

"A Quote By Mahatma Gandhi". *Goodreads.Com*, 2019. https://www.goodreads.com/quotes/24499-be-the-change-that-you-wish-to-see-in-the.

Pitofsky, Marina. "'It's Just Not For Me': Why A Growing Number Of Women Are Saying No To Parenthood". *Usatoday.Com*, 2019. https://www.usatoday.com/story/news/nation/2019/03/29/childfree-women-parenting-parenthood-no-kids/3153546002/.

Chapter 5

a Lionsgate presentation ; in association with Great American Films Limited Partnership ; produced by Linda Gottlieb ; written by Eleanor Bergstein ; directed by Emile Ardolino. *Dirty Dancing.* Santa Monica, Calif. :Lionsgate, 2010.

Chapter 6

Lyrics.com, STANDS4 LLC, 2019. "Better Together Lyrics." Accessed June 2, 2019. https://www.lyrics.com/lyric/26057381/Jack+Johnson.

Chapter 7

Anderson, Stuart. "10 Things You Need To Know About Ironman Triathlons". *Telegraph.Co.Uk*, 2015. https://www.telegraph.co.uk/men/active/11904053/10-things-you-need-to-know-about-Ironman-triathlons.html.

Deschene, Lori. "To Protect Your Energy". *Tiny Buddha*, 2019. https://tinybuddha.com/fun-and-inspiring/to-protect-your-energy/.

Chapter 8

Goldberg, Joel. "It Takes A Village To Determine The Origins Of An African Proverb". *Npr.Org*, 2016. https://www.npr.

org/sections/goatsandsoda/2016/07/30/487925796/it-takes-a-village-to-determine-the-origins-of-an-african-proverb.

Chapter 9

Horizon. "The Poison That Waits." Season 25, Episode 3. Valerie Palmer and colleagues. BBC, January 16, 1989. https://vimeo.com/1621281

"Nelson Mandela." In *Oxford Essential Quotations,* edited by Ratcliffe, Susan. : Oxford University Press, https://www.oxfordreference.com/view/10.1093/acref/9780191843730.001.0001/q-oro-ed5-00007046.

Chapter 10

espnW.com. "Study: Women + Sports = Executive Success". *ESPN.Com,* 2014. https://www.espn.com/espnw/w-in-action/story/_/id/11669072/women-+-sports-=-executive-success.

Torres Burtka, Allison. "Studies Show Athletes Bring Leadership Skills To The Work Place". *Globalsport Matters,* 2018. https://globalsportmatters.com/culture/2018/07/10/studies-show-athletes-bring-leadership-skills-work-place/.

Zemeckis, Robert, Steve Tisch, Wendy Finerman, Steve Starkey, Eric Roth, Don Burgess, Arthur Schmidt, et al. 2001. *Forrest Gump.* Hollywood, CA: Paramount Pictures

Chapter 11

Curtin, Melanie. "A 15-Year Study Of 5,000 Entrepreneurs Finally Answers The Question: Is It Better To Quit Your Day Job Or Keep It?". *Thriveglobal.Com*, 2018. https:// thriveglobal.com/stories/a-15-year-study-of-5-000-entrepreneurs-finally-answers-the-question-is-it-better-to-quit-your-day-job-or-keep-it/.

Raffiee, Joseph and Jie Feng. "Should I Quit My Day Job?: A Hybrid Path To Entrepreneurship | Academy of Management Journal". *Journals.Aom.Org*, 2013. https://journals.aom.org/doi/abs/10.5465/amj.2012.0522.

Solt, Andrew, Sam Egan, and Yōko Ono. 1988. *Imagine: John Lennon.* New York: Macmillan Pub. Co.

Chapter 12

Hollis, Rachel. *Girl, Wash Your Face.* Nelson Books, 2018.

Acknowledgements

Huge shout out to my family for supporting me through every step of this process and always encouraging me to pursue my dreams. Thank you for your time spent reading, tear-drying, and cheerleading from start to finish. Mom, Dad, and Lindsey – I love you and could not have done this without you.

This book would not exist without the following incredible women who allowed me the great honor of telling their stories. Their authenticity and vulnerability are awe-inspiring. It is a privilege to know you all. Thank you for your trust and your guidance!

Jean Thompson   Nancy Outcalt   Jenn Leitch

Kimberly DellaTorre	Melinda Thomas	Jill Boltmann
Jen Wisbey	Carolyn Kelly	Shannon Vetto
Christine Baerwaldt	Suzanne Salzberg	JoAnne Kennedy
Colleen Richey	Kalee Tyson	Jane (name changed)
Julie Johns	Mychele Riddick	Laurel Duquette
Laurie Black	Valerie Palmer	Mary Ellen Collentine
Gwen Sheridan	Gillian Crismier	Elaine Gibbons
Jess McMahon	Chelsey White	Kelsey Woods
Mollie Suits	Caroline Reis	Haley Katsman

A huge thank you to the following women who gifted me their time and shared their stories with me as well. I cherish our conversations and the wisdom you've kindly shared with me. I am so appreciative of your support. Thank you for sharing a slice of your world and connecting me with your networks. Can't wait to share these incredible stories in future projects!

Stephanie Sharrer	Wendy Kelley	Kate Alexander
Mary Herche	Alicia Scalzo Wilmoth	Allie Benson
Erin Hubert	Robin Schwartz	Jocelin Engel

Connie Amos	Sunny Pepin	Tia Cantrell
Leslie Scott	Camilla Fogle	Lisa Stewart
Tracy Wilkinson	Leslie Decker	Cindy Riccardo
Ann Marie Mulholland	Kerry Odeman	Susan Heiser

Thank you to everyone who believed in me enough to pre-order my book! You all helped make this dream become a reality and without you this book would not be here today. Your support and encouragement throughout this process has had a major impact on the final product. I can't thank you enough for your support. I am sincerely grateful for your help and hope to pay it forward one day.

SuperFauntie (Super Fan)	Meg, Scott, & Lindsey Dudley (Super Fan)	Virginia Vaughan Saldich (Super Fan)
Joy Dudley	The Family of Tad & Ellie Thomas	Tim & Kaye Zabrycki
Marshall Lee	Janet Dudley & Peter Griffin	Tom & Mary Thomas
The Stan Thomas Family	Mike Kury	The Taylor Family
Lori & Doug Greener	Eric Koester	Emma Schweiger
DeeDee Thompson	Debi Koenig	Elizabeth Fabozzi
Erika Guzman	Lori Blake	

Last but not least, thank you to Eric Koester for inviting me on the adventure of a lifetime to write and publish my first book. It has been an incredible journey, thank you for seeing and encouraging my potential. Thank you to Brian Bies and the publishing team at New Degree press – your guidance and reassurance throughout this process propelled me over the finish line. Thank you to my incredible editing team, Cortni Merritt, Elina Oliferovskiy, and Tracy Seybold, for helping me iterate and elevate each draft. This book would only be a fraction of what it is today without your expertise. Thank you to anyone else who had a hand in *Dream Smaller* I am so grateful for all of the help and support along the way!

Author Biography

When Drew Caitlin Dudley is not writing inspirational non-fiction, she is working on short fiction pieces, practicing her love for cooking, and wandering around Seattle in search of the best craft beer.

Ambitious and fearless, she was skiing double black diamonds at the age of 10 — upgrading to overseas vacations more recently. Drew took on the adventure of writing her first book with the same passion and dedication she gives her to her full-time sales career. Drew's conversational tone peppers *Dream Smaller*; you get the feeling that you're sitting in a cafe having coffee with Drew while she gives you the boost in spirit that any hard-working businesswoman/entrepreneur/mama/goal-setter may need from time to time.

CPSIA information can be obtained
at www.ICGtesting.com
Printed in the USA
FSHW021124221219
65366FS